Agents of Change

Agents of Change:
Scots in Poland, 1800–1918

MONA KEDSLIE McLEOD

TUCKWELL PRESS

First published in Great Britain in 2000 by
Tuckwell Press
The Mill House
Phantassie
East Linton
East Lothian EH40 3DG
Scotland

ISBN 1 86232 081 0

British Library Cataloguing-in-Publication Data
A catalogue record for this book is available
from the British Library

Typeset in Monotype Bembo by Carnegie Publishing, Lancaster
Printed and bound by The Cromwell Press, Trowbridge, Wiltshire

Contents

List of Illustrations

Acknowledgements

For the generosity of their hospitality and help with research in Poland I should like to thank Dr Jerzy Naziębło, Peter Pininski, Alexander Radjay, Professor Jerzy Szczepański, Dr Margaret Hay and the many historians, to whom they introduced me, who were able to answer my questions. For help in Scotland I should like to thank the Consuls General in Edinburgh and Dr Simon Niziol. Zbigniew Budinski translated innumerable Polish documents for me and my sister, Mary Biedermann, wrestled successfully with the German of Karl Dittrich's report. Mary Burkett made a major contribution to the success of my second visit to Poland as an indomitable companion and tireless photographer. Iseabeal Macleod read the text with meticulous care and to her and to my husband, Robert Lewis, I am deeply grateful for much constructive criticism. Without Robert's patient support the book could not have been written. I am also grateful to Peter Gunn for preparing the index.

I would also like to thank the following for permission to reproduce illustrations:

Mary Burkett: 1, 3, 4, 6, 8, 10, 11, 19, 20, 21, 24, 27, 28, 43, 64, 65. Pallas Guides: 2, 23, 27. National Galleries of Scotland: 5. Patricia Stephen: 7. John Dewar: 9. Instytut Sztuki, Warsaw: 14, 22, 26, 29, 30. I G Anderson: 15. Enid Gauldie: 33. Muzeum Okregowe w Zyrardowie: 34, 35, 36, 37, 48, 49, 50, 51, 52, 55, 56, 61. The illustrations that appear on pages 12, 13, 16, 18, 25, 31, 32, 38, 39, 40, 41, 42, 44, 45, 46, 53, 54, 57, 58, 59, 60, 62, 63, 66 and 67 are my own.

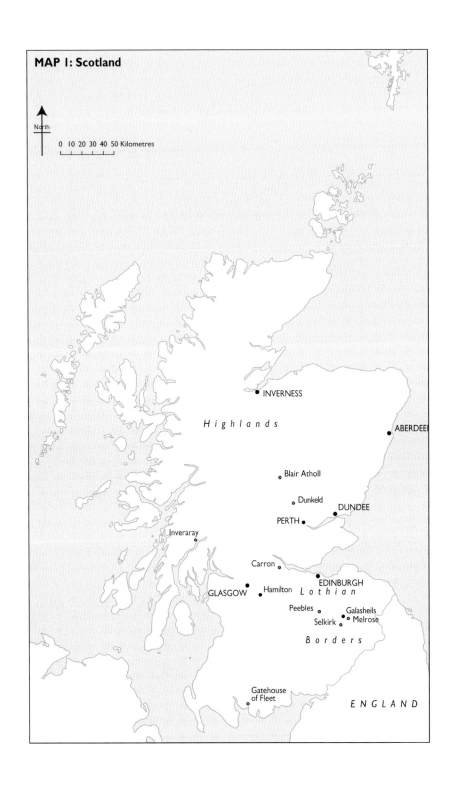

MAP I: Scotland

North

0 10 20 30 40 50 Kilometres

INVERNESS

Highlands

ABERDEEN

Blair Atholl

Dunkeld

DUNDEE

PERTH

Inveraray

Carron

EDINBURGH

GLASGOW Hamilton *Lothian*

Peebles Galasheils
Selkirk Melrose

Borders

Gatehouse
of Fleet

ENGLAND

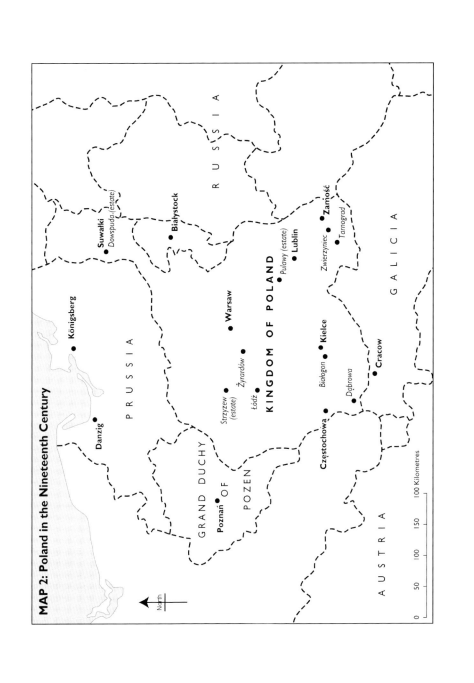

MAP 2: Poland in the Nineteenth Century

Introduction

As a family, we grew up in England, knowing that we were the purest of pure Scots, but there was always a Polish presence in the house. In the dining room, a portrait of Grandfather Garvie, a distinguished old gentleman with a white beard, hung over the fireplace and on the opposite wall was a picture of the linen factory in Żyrardów in which he had been a partner and a senior director. A vast sideboard carved by some Polish Grinling Gibbons dominated the room. At table Granny Garvie spoke to my mother in Polish and she replied in English. Janka Govenlock, a distant relative and a refugee from the Russian Revolution, presided in the kitchen. A formidable figure, the terror of errant message boys, she never learnt to speak English and my father never spoke Polish. We children understood a little but spoke less.

Tension was never far from the surface, but on Christmas Eve Poland took over. For weeks, cards would have been arriving which were unmistakably different from British ones and there was always a parcel with Christmas wafers – rice paper embossed with scenes from the Nativity – and dried fruits to make a compôte for the Fast Supper. In the morning a vast table, its central support four swans carved by the same Polish craftsman, was extended to take twenty people. The cloth, part of my grandmother's trousseau, was set with china from Bohemia, glass from Venice and silver from Russia. The tree was decorated and candles lit before Santa Claus arrived to give us our presents and then, Scotland represented only by my father's and brother's kilts, we went through to the dining room for supper. Family and friends, we all stood behind our chairs till Granny, a tiny figure in black satin and lace, had broken a corner of the wafers with each and given us the Christmas greeting.

Supper was always the same. The Polish beetroot soup borsch, served with mashed potatoes, was followed by fish and a wonderful sauce which I remember as being mainly butter and hardboiled eggs. Though traditionally carp, in Leeds in the 1930s it was more often a large cod.

The meal ended with a compôte of dried fruits and a rare opportunity to eat as many nuts and sugared almonds as we wanted. It was bedtime before we became British again, hung up our stockings and looked forward to turkey and Christmas pudding the next day.

Who were these Hays, Dicksons and Govenlocks, Czarlinskis, Grabowskis and Hannichs from whom the cards had come? Why had they gone to Poland and why were so many of them still there? By the time I tried to find out my mother had died, but she had the instincts and training of an historian. It was amongst the letters, memoirs and notebooks which her parents had brought back with them in 1906, and she had preserved, that I found the first clues in the hunt for my Scottish ancestors in Poland.

Pursuing them, I discovered that they were only part of a much larger community of staunchly Presbyterian Scots who had emigrated to Poland between 1815 and 1830. Engineers, farmers, weavers and millers, highly skilled and highly literate, they left Scotland reluctantly, driven by the fear or reality of financial failure. By comparison with Scotland, where the economy had been devastated by the depression which followed the collapse of markets at the end of the Napoleonic Wars, the newly created Congress Kingdom of Poland seemed a land of promise. But, in 1825, the liberal but always unstable Czar Alexander I was suceeded as king of Poland by the reactionary Nicholas I. Russian misrule led to the 1830 Rising and its failure to the destruction of the Kingdom and the death or exile of the most enterprising of the Polish upper classes. Without their support, and usually under-capitalised, several Scottish ventures collapsed in the hostile economic climate deliberately created by the repressive Russian government. But the survivors held on. By the 1860s farmers were becoming landowners, foremen became managers, and managers directors.

It was into this closely knit, Protestant, intermarried and relatively wealthy community of Scots that my mother was born in 1885. At least 200 must have been relatives. They had revolutionised farming on the Pac and Zamoyski estates, trained hundreds of Polish technicians in the factories they owned or managed and, at Żyrardów, had helped to create a model industrial town as well as a textile factory which produced the finest linen in Europe. They had become bankers, doctors, nurses and entrepreneurs, a part of the increasingly important middle class. By the end of the nineteenth century the province of Poland had become the most economically advanced in the Russian empire. The 1914–18 War and the Bolshevik Revolution destroyed the economy and, in the political chaos of the twentieth century, the Scottish contribution to the prosperity of Poland in the nineteenth century has been forgotten. Starting from family papers, I have tried to discover who these Scots were, what they did and how they lived in a country in which so many of them remained strangers.

CHAPTER ONE

Why Poland?

By the thirteenth century Scottish contacts with the Baltic were well established. Westerly winds took the enterprising trader from the limited markets of Scotland to the apparently unlimited opportunities of mainland Europe. These were the men whom William Wallace was recommending to the burghers of Lübeck in 1297, traders in fish, salt and hides with return cargoes of timber and corn. Too often, however, they were followed by hordes of penniless young men. By the fifteenth century they were being linked in Poland with 'Jews and other vagabonds': in France with vermin!

> Mark you what the proverb says
> > Of Scotsmen, rats and lice
> The whole world over, take your ways,
> > You'll find them still I guess.

There were, in fact, substantial colonies of Scottish merchants settled abroad, supplying the Flemish textile industry with wool from the flocks of the Border abbeys but there was little room for the Scotsman and his pedlar's pack in the relatively advanced economies of medieval France or the Netherlands. He was excluded from the cities of Germany by the Hanseatic League and it was only in Poland that he readily found a place. In a country of aristocrats, debarred by rank from trade or the professions, and peasants trapped in poverty by their status as serfs, a hawker might become a merchant and a merchant a very rich man. Danzig, a city free from the restrictive control of the Hanseatic League, gave him entry into a country with a long record for toleration of foreigners. Since its union with Lithuania in 1386 it had also become one of the largest markets in Europe. Poland became 'The Heaven of the nobility, the Paradise for the Jews, the Hell for the peasant and the gold-mine for the stranger'.

By the sixteenth century the trickle of Scottish emigrants had become a flood. The Elizabethan traveller, Fynes Moryson, wrote:

1 Warsaw: Merchant's House in the Old Town. Trading from Aberdeen or Leith,
Scottish merchants entered Poland through the free port of Danzig and formed
Brotherhoods in the towns in which they settled. Alexander Chalmers, a member of
the Warsaw Brotherhood, was thrice elected provost of the city in the 1690s.

The Scots flock in great numbers into Poland ... rather from the
poverty of their own kingdom than for any great traffic they
exercised there, dealing rather for small fardels than for great
quantities of rich wares.[1]

The report of Patrick Gordon, the Scots consul in Danzig, confirms
the picture of the poverty of many of the immigrants. His complaint
about the scandal caused by 'boys incapable of service and destitute
of means of living ... many times dying in the streets' led to legislation
by James VI to prevent the emigration of unsponsored youths.[2] This
may have had some success, since established merchants were as hostile
to impecunious newcomers as was the consul.

There is ample evidence for the success of many of the earlier
merchants. From 1576 Polish kings who valued their services had

2. The New Town, Warsaw: Copernicus Statue. Poland was economically
backward but she had a rich cultural history. Under Stanisław August, her last king,
Warsaw became a brilliant capital city.

granted rights of self-government to communities of Scots and James VI
had ordered them to form Brotherhoods to which all Scottish merchants
were to be admitted.[3] In twelve towns like Zamość, Lublin and Cracow
these were established with their own churches, courts, judges and
charities. Eight of the most successful merchants, 'The Scots who
always follow our court ... Our Court cannot be without them, that
supply us with all that is necessary', were appointed 'Merctores Aulici'
– purveyors and bankers to the crown. If they could produce birth-
brieves to establish their status as gentlemen in Scotland, Scots could
be accepted into the Polish upper classes; some, like the banker
Fergusson, were enobled. In the seventeenth century Lublin had two
Scottish mayors and Alexander Chalmers, a linen merchant, was three
times mayor of Warsaw; Alexander Cockburn's fortune founded an
art gallery and a technical school in Danzig; Robert Brown of Zamość
established a scholarship at Edinburgh University for one Polish and
one Scottish student and Robert Gordon brought his fortune home
to found Robert Gordon's College in Aberdeen. In the eighteenth
century the first church built for the Protestant community in Warsaw
was financed by a Fergusson.

The mercenary soldiers, who in the seventeenth century fought with the Poles against Swedes, Turks and Russians, formed another large group. General Patrick Gordon – 'the younger son of a younger brother of a minor branch of the family' – was typical. Writing in 1669, he complained that 'Even in Scotland soldiers of fortune can attain no honourable employment'. Though a Catholic, he would have preferred to pursue his military career in Protestant Scotland. Few of the common soldiers survived to return. Many, like Gordon, were as likely to be fighting for the Swedes as against them. They followed the wars across northern Europe, finding employment where they could. In Russia Gordon became a friend of Peter the Great and one of the founders of his army. But the men who raised and commanded the companies employed by the Polish kings were often from landed families to whom Catholicism was more important than it appears to have been to Gordon. These were likely to marry into the Polish upper classes and were rapidly assimilated into their society. From both these highly literate groups of merchants and retired officers, senior officials were recruited to serve the magnates and the crown.

William Lithgow, the distinguished linguist and traveller from Clydeside who reached Poland in 1616, wrote:

> Here I found abundance of gallant rich merchants, my countrymen, who were all very kind to me ... And for auspiciousness I may rather term it to be a Mother and Nurse, for the youth and younglings of Scotland who are yearly sent here in great numbers than a proper Dame for her own birth: in clothing, feeding and enriching them with the fatness of her best things, beside 30,000 Scots families that live incorporate in her bowels. And certainly Poland may be termed in this kind to be the mother of our Commons and the first commencement of all our best merchant's wealth or at least most part of them.[4]

Lithgow's startling figure of 30,000 is generally accepted by historians. The emigrants were believed to be so prosperous that Charles II – an impecunious refugee in the Netherlands – tried, with limited success, to tax them for his support.[5] In 1670 the governor of Jamaica requested that 'all prudential means be used to encourage the Scots to come hither ... and to prevent them going to Poland and other foreign nations'.[6] And it was to America that, after 1707, the Scots were to emigrate in their thousands. As separate communities, with their own churches and guilds, the Scots in Poland were to disappear. Of Poland at the end of the eighteenth century Francis Steuart wrote:

> Here and there, in Polish farms and manors, you could still meet a 'Douglas', a 'Lendze' or an 'Ogilvy' who, though he had no papers to prove it, says he knows his forbears came from Caledonia.[7]

A few surnames survived – Hay and Dickson – but most were polonised; MacLeod became Machlejd, Cockburn Kabron and Keith Keitz. Many married Poles and converted to Catholicism. Why, in the early nineteenth century, did significant numbers again turn to Poland?

Early settlers had often been adventurers but in the nineteenth century Scots went to Poland by invitation. The role of the Polish landed aristocracy was critical. The most privileged group in Europe, they had, by the seventeenth century, monopolised politics and control of the economy. In Britain the class structure was flexible. Impoverished gentry and younger sons could turn to trade or the professions to improve their finances without losing status; a successful entrepreneur could buy an estate and become a gentleman. William Forbes, a younger son who had made a fortune in the Danzig timber trade, invested it in the lands and barony on which he built Craigievar in Aberdeenshire in the 1620s. The Clerks of Penicuik were descended from successful merchants in Edinburgh and Paris. In Poland the system was rigid. The landowners, the *szlachta*, were frequently so impoverished that they had to sell their estates, but if they engaged in productive work they lost their status and were disenfranchised. As late as 1835 an American visitor to Poland could write in his *Incidents of Travel in Greece, Turkey and Poland*: 'They consider it a disgrace to practice any profession, even law and medicine'.[8] Paid employment was only possible in the household of one of the magnates, or in the church. The great families, the Czartoryskis, the Radziwills or the Zamoyskis, formed the richest and most powerful aristocracy in Europe; the lesser landowners the poorest. Farming the land were the peasants, most of them still serfs without civil rights. Towns, with the exception of the

3. Polish plough. The primitive wooden plough which could only scratch the ground was still used by Polish peasants in the nineteenth century. From J. C. Loudon's *Book of the Farm*, 1831.

free city of Danzig, had no representation in the parliament and successful merchants, whether Jews or gentiles, were unable to buy the land which alone could have given them political power. In these conditions a prosperous middle class could not develop.

In 1530 the monarchy had become elective. Any landowner was eligible for election and successive candidates made concession after concession to win votes. Like the Holy Roman Emperor, the King of Poland became powerless. The 'Liberum Veto' enabled any member of the parliament, however ignorant or poverty-stricken, to cancel the entire work of the session, and, without parliamentary consent, neither new laws nor taxes could be introduced. By the eighteenth century the Republic of Nobles had become ungovernable. Controlled by the landowners, the economy of what had, in the sixteenth century, been one of the richest nations in Europe declined. A paralysis set in which 'eventually led to stagnation and then catastrophe'.[9]

To eighteenth-century travellers it was a country of stark contrasts. David Hume thought it was the most backward state in Europe: Bernardin de Saint-Pierre wrote: 'Nowhere is there a more magnificent nobility, and nowhere such bad citizens'. Others were impressed by the brilliance of Warsaw society and the magnificence of the houses of the magnates but appalled by the state of the roads, the inns and the farming. Only half the land was cultivated and productivity was one sixth of that of land in England.[10] Although there were four universities and ten academies, education was controlled by Jesuits still steeped in the theology and philosophy of the Counter-Reformation. Figures for illiteracy are startling. In the early eighteenth century, in a population of ten million, 18% of the magnates, 40% of the middle nobility, 92% of the petty nobility and 40% of the burghers are believed to have been illiterate.[11] Ignorance and bigotry were widespread.

The Enlightenment and the reign of Poland's last king, Stanisław August Poniatowski (1764–93), came too late to prevent disaster. For thirty years after he was elected, King Stanisław tried to reform the constitution and rejuvenate the economy. The rigidity of the class system was diminished so that a powerful urban community could develop; between 1760 and 1792 the population of Warsaw increased from 30,000 to 150,000. He encouraged new industries by improving banking and communications and bringing foreign experts and technologies into the country. On his own estates he introduced improved farming and industries related to agriculture; the most intelligent of the magnates and churchmen followed his example. The Czartoryskis imported craftsmen from Sèvres to teach workers in their porcelain factory at Korzec, and Prince Michael Ogiński planned a canal to link the Baltic with the Black Sea. Productivity soared. The Commission for Education, which was set up in 1774, was the first of its kind in Europe. It recognised that a system of general and technical education, divorced from church control, was essential to progress. This was a reform which struck at the roots of Polish backwardness and, had it been given time, might have transformed the economy of the kingdom.

During Poniatowski's reign the sons of aristocrats like the Czartoryskis, the Potockis and the Zamoyskis, began to extend their Grand Tours from England to Scotland and visited universities and factories as well as the great houses of the nobility. Jan Sniadecki, who later became the principal of Vilnius University, was in Edinburgh from 1793 to 1796. After studying medicine under James Gregory, Andrew Duncan and Alexander Monro he described the University as 'a seat of true philosophy, cleansed of misconceptions, preconceptions and exaggeration'.[12] The philosophical pragmatism of the Scottish Enlightenment played a dominant role in the development of Polish thought

4. The Ordynacja. The administrative centre of the vast Zamoyski estates in south-east Poland.

and the creation of an intellectual elite ready to support Poniatowski. The publication of Sniadecki's *Philosophy of the Human Mind*, in 1822, made the work of the Scottish philosophers and scientists, Adam Smith in particular, familiar to the generation of Poles who were to initiate economic developments in the Congress Kingdom.

Tragically, Poniatowski's reforms roused the opposition not only of the most reactionary of the landowners and churchmen but also of Poland's neighbours. The country might have become both prosperous and governable; Russia, Prussia and Austria were determined that she should be neither. Catherine the Great, Frederick of Prussia and the Austrian autocrats Elizabeth and Joseph, were prepared to play with the ideas of the Enlightenment as long as democracy was kept safely at bay. They saw the Constitution of 1791 as a threat to absolutism in their own countries. Based on American and English political theory, it gave Poland an hereditary monarchy limited by an elected parliament and judiciary. The Liberum Veto was abolished and the king's executive power increased. Illiterate and landless members of the *szlachta* were disenfranchised, towns were represented and a Third Estate of substantial property owners was created. Those peasants who were still serfs were given civil rights. The Constitution, the most liberal in eighteenth-century Europe, was welcomed by democratic thinkers in western Europe. Karl Marx's comment, made half a century later, is the most interesting:

> With all its faults, this constitution seems to be the only act of freedom which Eastern Europe has undertaken in the midst of Prussian, Russian and Austrian barbarism. It was, moreover, initiated exclusively by the privileged classes, the nobility. The history of the world knows no other example of similar noble conduct by the nobility.

The barbarians decided to destroy Poland as an independent state. The Partition of 1772 gave Russia a foothold in a country of great potential wealth whose frontiers were almost impossible to defend. Edward Burke foresaw the second stage: 'The Empress of Russia has breakfasted: when will she dine?' The Partitions of 1793 and 1795 wiped Poland off the map. Russia, for the first time in her history, became a major European power and Prussia gained territory on which she could build the economic base from which she was to dominate Germany.

Those aristocrats who had opposed the Constitution because it reduced their power and laid the foundations of a modern democratic state found themselves politically powerless. Still landowners, but under foreign rule, the more enterprising turned to the economy, the one field in which they could still operate. Their response was strikingly similar to that of the Scottish upper classes in 1707. The Union of the Parliaments deprived many of its members of an active political role. The magnates, Argyll and Bute and their circles, played the power game from London but those who stayed in Scotland became 'Improvers', pouring energy and capital into their estates. By 1720 'the Honourable the Society of Improvers' was encouraging the adoption of the most advanced farming techniques and was developing banking; its members invested in new industries and created model villages outside the walls of their newly enclosed parks. Rents soared, country houses proliferated and small farmers were replaced by 'gentlemen' farmers. Subsistence farming and short joint tenancies began to disappear and the enclosure movement turned the less successful peasant farmers into landless labourers. These 'Improvers' were the men whom the Czartoryskis, the Potockis, and the Zamoyskis met in Scotland as they toured the farms, factories and gardens of their hosts and the departments of science of the universities. Links were broken during the Napoleonic Wars when, as citizens of the Grand Duchy of Warsaw, Poles fought with the French against her arch-enemies, the partitioning powers and their ally Britain. But as soon as the Wars were over they and their sons were back in Scotland.

Napoleon's defeat destroyed all hope that Poland might recover her pre-1795 frontiers, and the Congress of Vienna divided her up once more. Cracow alone became a free state. Austria recovered Galicia; Prussia regained Silesia and the port of Danzig; Russia again got the lion's share. Out of it she created the Congress Kingdom. The relatively liberal czar, Alexander I, had been an admirer of Napoleon's reforms and accepted the constitution drawn up by Prince Adam Czartoryski, an Anglophile, an idealist, a friend of the czar's and the most powerful of the Polish magnates. This gave Poland a parliament, a council and some real autonomy. Control of army and police remained in Moscow but all other departments were in Warsaw. Russian markets were opened and there was a period of optimism during which the economy could expand and Polish institutions flourish. It was short-lived. By 1820 the parliament had been dismissed and in 1825 the reactionary Nicholas I succeeded his brother as king and czar. Every constitutional promise was broken and, by 1830, the Poles were driven into rebellion. The failure of the Rising reduced Poland to the status of a kingdom without a constitution and subjected her to the barbarity of military government.

It was from 1815 to 1830, during these early years of optimism, that a second generation of Polish landowners came to Scotland. Deeply impressed by the wealth of the estates they visited, they found agents who persuaded hundreds of Scots to emigrate, taking their skills as craftsmen, engineers and farmers with them. They were caught up in the period of economic depression and political repression which followed the failure of the Rising, but the majority stayed on to create the closely-knit Scottish communities which survived until the First World War.

Krystyn Lach Szyrma, in his *Reminiscences of a Journey through England and Scotland*, has left a wonderful record of how the early contacts were made.[13] Szyrma, who later became professor of Philosophy in the short-lived University of Warsaw, came to Scotland as tutor to the young princes Czartoryski and Sapieha in 1820. They were taught privately, at the considerable fee of £10 for each of the six students in the Polish group, by the distinguished economist J. R. McCulloch. Attending lectures at the University, Szyrma was fascinated by the wide range of age and class amongst the students:

> Here elderly men are not ashamed to attend lectures together with the very young, and a foreigner watching a white haired old man beside striplings makes a mental note that, in this Athens of the North, education is not finished early in life.

Of the student-run societies in which they discussed work and read their own papers, he wrote:

> This system develops their faculties of independent thinking ... in their discussions they are very fair to each other; their civility is exemplary and equality is respected.

At these meetings, he and his pupils would make contact with the sons and grandsons of 'Improvers', but in the company of a Czartoryski or a Sapieha all doors would in any case have been opened. Of the Duke of Hamilton, who had been an envoy to the court of Catherine the Great, he wrote: 'he is one of those nobles who invariably extend their hospitality and their protection to all Poles travelling in Scotland'. Dining with the Duke, he found the company included the writer Hogg, the painter Watson and the mathematician Leslie, all men whose social origins would have made them unlikely guests at the table of a Polish aristocrat. Visiting the estate of Lord Murray, he met one of his tenants, a Mr Muir from Kirkcudbright,

> who talked about agriculture, not like a farmer but like a professor, but with less conceit ... There is an exceptional equilibrium between the different social classes headed by the most cultured set.

At a time when the export of machinery from Britain was still restricted by law, Szyrma knew that he would have difficulty in wresting technical secrets from Scottish manufacturers. Even Robert Burns, on a literary tour in 1787, had been refused entry to the Carron Iron Works, where the first blast furnaces to be installed in Scotland were in operation. He recorded his experience in verse:

> We cam na here to view your works
>> In hopes to be mair wise
> But only, lest we gang to Hell,
>> It may be nae surprise.
>
> But when we tirled at your door
>> Your porter dought na bear us
> So may, should we to Hell yetts come,
>> Your billy Satan sair us.

Earlier in the century Mrs Henry Fletcher of Saltoun in East Lothian had been in a position similar to Szyrma's. Determined to improve the quality of linen being produced on the Fletcher estate, she visited the Netherlands. The two wheelwrights she took with her were dressed as lackeys. While Mrs Fletcher chatted with the owners of the Dutch textile factories she visited, her 'lackeys' made mental notes of the technical details of machines used to produce the finest linen in Europe. On their return to Scotland they set up machines capable of producing linen of a similar quality. Szyrma, a philosopher and an academic, pleaded ignorance of all things mechanical as he toured the factories of a rapidly industrialising Scotland. But, like the Saltoun wheelwrights, he made detailed notes and drawings of every machine or invention which he thought might be of use on a Polish estate. Of the people, he noted that:

> The high standard of education awakens a spirit of enterprise which makes many people emigrate later to England and America ... there are no peasants as in our country and no serfdom ... [the crofters are] the middle class, from whose homes come great clergymen and scholars ... the discoverers in the fields of mechanics and science, or again people who make great fortunes.

These were the Scots whom Szyrma's pupils were determined should emigrate to Poland, and not to England or America.

NOTES

1. A. F. Steuart, *Papers Relating to the Scots in Poland*, XIII.
2. *Ibid*, XIV.
3. *Ibid*, XIV.
4. *Ibid*, X.
5. *Ibid*, XVII.
6. I. C. C. Graham, *Colonists from Scotland*, 70.
7. A. F. Steuart, *op cit.*, 110.
8. W. Jasiakiewicz, in *Polish-Anglo Saxon Studies*, 6–7, 98.
9. A. Maczak, in *A Republic of Nobles*, 111.
10. A. Zamoyski, *The Last King of Poland*, 6.
11. A. Zamoyski, *The Polish Way*, 258.
12. S. Zabieglik, in *Polish-Anglo Saxon Studies*, 6–7, 73.
13. K. L. Szyrma, *Reminiscences of a Journey through England and Scotland 1823–24*, unpublished trans.

CHAPTER TWO

Lowland Scotland, 1790–1815

Had a Zamoyski or a Czartoryski visited Scotland in 1700, he would have found little to inspire him in the state of her economy. Some of the most enterprising of the landowners had started to enclose their estates and plant windbreaks round their castles but, in much of Scotland, he would have seen subsistence farming in a windswept landscape and industrial development checked by limited markets, primitive technologies and lack of capital. Attempts to enlarge Scotland's markets by founding a colony at Darien on the Isthmus of Panama had failed, what little capital she had had was lost in that disastrous venture and, in the 1690s, thousands had died of starvation after a series of crop failures and late harvests. Most significantly, he would have observed Scotsmen who, in the words of Sir John Clerk of Penicuik, were 'Resigned to sit down under all these misfortunes and, in a kind of glade poverty, live on what remained.'

A hundred years later the scene had been transformed. Clerk, one of the first of the improving landowners, believed that only by union with England could Scotland break out of her poverty. The Union of 1707 opened up what had been the English Empire to the Scots and, by mid-century, capital accumulated in colonial trade was being ploughed back into the Scottish economy. Landowners, on their increasingly frequent journeys to London, were stimulated by what they saw of English economic developments to enclose and improve their own estates. By the end of the century windbreaks in the Lothians were sheltering some of the finest land in Britain and Scots were developing some of the most advanced farming techniques in Europe. The textile industry was manufacturing everything from fine damask to sailcloth and carpets; the iron industry was producing the machines an industrialising nation needed as well as armaments for her own and her allies' armed forces. Canals transformed both the speed and the cost of transport in the central belt, and the network of roads which now extended to the Highlands made travel, for the first time in

Scottish history, relatively easy. Carriages and carts were replacing packhorses and sledges; harbours were being built and enlarged.

Underlying the expanding economy was a banking system which provided loan capital at relatively low interest rates. The Bank of Scotland, founded in 1696, soon had competitors in the Royal Bank and the British Linen Company. Established in 1746 'to do everything that may conduce to the promoting and carrying on of the linen industry', it became a chartered bank providing working capital for a growing industry. Private banks associated with other industries followed. At a time when companies in England were limited to six partners, joint-stock companies with up to 60 partners with limited liability were legal in Scotland. They could afford to take risks and, if involved in overseas trade, set up agencies in ports like Königsberg and Danzig as well as throughout the British Isles. By the end of the eighteenth century, Scotland was served by a network of banks competing to make credit available for the enterprising.

The enterprising, men able to invent, initiate and take advantage of opportunities, were the product of the Scottish educational system. Closely linked to Scotland's Calvinist church were the parish schools which tried to ensure that all children, however poor, should be able to read the Bible. Although not compulsory, it was socially unacceptable not to send your children to school. Fees were within the reach of a working man. In 1790 a minister in Dumfriesshire reckoned that a farm labourer whose family income amounted to about £20 a year would have to spend 10/- annually to send his four children to school.[1] Landowners – the heritors – were expected to pay the fees of the poorest children in the parish. The schoolmasters were almost invariably graduates, competent to teach Latin, French and mathematics to any child whose parents could pay a few extra shillings. Perhaps more important, they were able to recognise high ability and might persuade the heritors to finance a gifted child through grammar school and university. Grammar schools in the towns provided the classical grounding necessary for university education, and many of the newer academies included modern languages, book-keeping, navigation, surveying and sciences in their curricula. In Glasgow the Anderson Institute was the first of many technical colleges which made it possible for a working man to study part-time, while in Edinburgh, in the

5. Sir John Sinclair, 1754–1835, by Sir Henry Raeburn. *The Statistical Account of Scotland 1791–99*, which Sinclair edited, described the conditions which produced the highly skilled engineers and farmers who emigrated in the early years of the nineteenth century. He visited Poland, where his writings on agriculture were known and admired, in 1786.

6. George Rennie's gravestone at Preston Kirk, East Linton. Landowners came from many parts of Europe to study the advanced farming methods practiced by Rennie at Phantassie in East Lothian.

School of Arts, Lach Szyrma found 425 artisans being trained by master craftsmen. In the evenings they could study Newton and Davy in their own homes, borrowing books from public libraries.'Those who are less well off hire books and this can be done even in the smallest town.'[2] With the universities the Poles were already familiar; the parents of Szyrma's pupils had all attended classes at Edinburgh in the eighteenth century. St Andrews had a collegiate system but at Glasgow, Aberdeen and Edinburgh students usually found their own accommodation. This made it possible, for those who could survive on porridge and minimal heating, to get through an academic year on about £30. For wealthy students who boarded with professors the cost could be several hundreds.

The Poles were particularly attracted to Edinburgh by the pragmatism of the teaching. After attending classes there Szyrma wrote:

> It must be stated to the glory of this university that, great though the development of heart and mind through ideas might be, it has always been the aim of the University to adapt learning to life and make it practical ... Misery is being fought here by education ... Well educated, they know how to adapt their ways of living to their means ... The high educational standards and iron endurance of the Scots will be surpassed by no one.[3]

Fees at every stage were low. In the south of Scotland literacy was normal and a higher education was possible for many.

What must have struck the Poles who visited Scotland at the beginning of the nineteenth century was the extent to which initiative had come from the landowners. They had improved their own farms first and then, by 'improving' leases, the farms of their tenants. Short joint tenancies were replaced by long leases on enclosed farms. During the early rent-free years the tenant had to drain his land and build dykes with the stones lifted off his fields. Rents could then be trebled and money invested in planned villages, rural industries and turnpike trusts. Mansions replaced towers and solid stone-built farmhouses the hovels of the old ferm touns. In the country the worst social effects of industrialisation were still to come and New Lanark, Deanston and Gatehouse of Fleet could be seen as model industrial villages. In the climate created by the reforms which pre-dated the Partitions of Poland,

Scotland could and did provide an inspiration and example to the most intelligent of the Polish landowners. Their sons were to follow in their footsteps.

The country they saw has been described with great clarity in the *First Statistical Account of Scotland*. In 1790 Sir John Sinclair, a man of insatiable curiosity and the president of the newly formed Board of Agriculture, sent to the ministers of the Church of Scotland a questionnaire with 166 questions relating to the economic and social state of their parishes. Many of the ministers were shrewd observers. 'Moderates' in their religious beliefs and farming their own glebe lands, they were probably more interested in agriculture and the daily lives of their parishioners than in the finer points of theological controversy. The changes which had taken place within the previous 40 years were meticulously described. A clear picture of the Lothians and the Tweed valley, from which so many Scots were to emigrate twenty years later, emerges. Of farming in the parish of Melrose the Rev George Thomson wrote:

> Within these thirty years the farmers have made vast progress in agriculture. Through their unremitting industry, a great quantity of ground, formerly covered with heath, broom and furze, has been bared and now produces excellent crops or is converted into good pasture. The value of the land has consequently very much increased. A feu of several hundred acres, purchased about 40 years ago at £10, was lately sold at the advanced price of £150 sterling. The parish is supposed to produce double the amount of grain it did about that time. The manure used is lime, marl and dung . . .[4]

In the neighbouring parish of Galashiels the Rev Robert Douglas reported that 17 wrights had substantial businesses manufacturing agricultural implements as well as their normal engineering and carpentry activities. On one estate alone, six large farmhouses and steadings had been built; there were 32 good new dwelling houses in the village and 39 outside it.[5] What had been a village was becoming a small industrial town. When depression hit agriculture 25 years later Douglas' grandson, William Hay, was one of a colony of Scots farmers who emigrated from the Borders to General Pac's Dowspuda estate in north-east Poland.

7. Phantassie, *c.* 1820. General Chłapowski and the Zamoyski brothers stayed at Phantassie. They learnt to plough with Small's swing plough and to build stacks which could store corn and hay out-of-doors at minimal cost.

In East Lothian, winds off the North Sea had retarded growth. The parish of Tyninghame and Whitekirk caught the full force of the blast. Mr James Williams describes its transformation from sandhills and rabbit warrens to some of the finest farmland in Europe. In 1700 a German guest with similarly windswept estates on the Baltic coast had persuaded the Countess of Haddington, though not her husband, that a windbreak could be created:

> Fourteen acres were planted, it being supposed that no trees could grow because of the sea air and the North East winds. The Earl at first either believed the common opinion or had no turn for planting: but his Lady being an active woman began; when her success was observed, the Earl entered keenly into her plans ...[6]

A thousand acres of woodland were planted and, behind this massive windbreak, farming flourished. By the 1790s the minister of Athelstaneford, a few miles from the coast, could write:

The lands of the parish are, in general, in a high state of cultivation and produce rich crops of every species of grain, particularly of wheat, barley and oats. The introduction of drilled crops, which happened within the last 30 years, has been of singular use in this parish ... Besides turnips, a quantity of potatoes is raised which is a great blessing to the lower class of people ...[7]

Farms were from 50 to 500 acres and Athelstaneford became a model village of substantial stone houses and cottages.

By the last decades of the century, the curved iron mouldboards of James Small's ploughs were producing fine deep tilths and Andrew Meikle's threshing machines were being widely used. The labour-intensive threshing floors became redundant, as did the wooden ploughs and ox teams which had, for centuries, inefficiently scratched the surface of the soil. A ploughman and his two Clydesdale horses could do the work of three men and eight oxen. Sinclair, who, in one of his fact-finding missions, had visited Denmark, Sweden, Russia, Poland, Austria, Prussia, the Netherlands and France, wrote:

There is perhaps no country in Europe in which implements of husbandry have been brought to such perfection, simplicity of form and excellence of execution as in Scotland.[8]

Although the initiative had come from the landowners, Sinclair, himself an improver from Caithness in the far north, had no doubt about the importance of the role of the farmer. He concluded:

Proprietors may turn up and adorn a few acres around their own mansions but it is the judicious, diligent and persevering efforts of the husbandman alone which can extend improvements on a grand scale and render them lasting and beneficial to the public.[9]

These were the tenant farmers who were able to respond to increased demand for corn and beef during the French wars. Prices soared — corn from 50/– a quarter in 1794 to 126/6 in 1812 and beef from £2 a beast in 1786 to £18 in 1814. Rents went up too, and leases were sometimes shortened so that landowners could benefit more rapidly from rising prices. By 1815 rents were probably eight times the mid-eighteenth century level. Farmers on the best land could pay

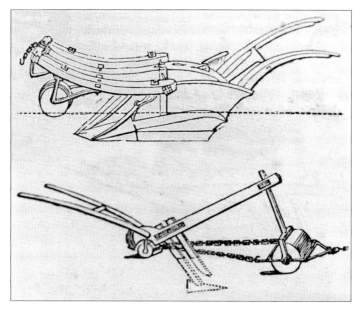

8. Improved ploughs. Two of the many ploughs in use in the
Lothians. From Alexander Kedslie's copy of J. C. Loudon's *Encyclopedia
of Agriculture.*

and prosper. It was those who farmed marginal land who would be
ruined when prices collapsed at the end of the wars.

In industry, too, the initiative had often come from the landowners.
In 1727 the Board of Commissioners for Manufactures had made
bounties available for employment of foreign craftsmen and purchase
of machinery. On their own estates they built breweries, distilleries,
paper and sawmills to absorb surplus agricultural produce and attract
tradesmen to their villages. Gatehouse of Fleet in Galloway was typical
of the second stage of industrialisation, when factories were set up in
the country which depended on imported raw materials and new
technologies. The landowner, James Murray of Broughton, brought
experts from Ulster and Yorkshire to help him to establish a cotton-
spinning mill at the mouth of the Fleet river. The river was dredged
to provide water power from a loch formed up river and a harbour
was created at the estuary. To service the cotton mill a brass foundry,
a machine shop, two tanneries, a soapworks and two breweries were
founded. Robert Heron, after touring the south-west in 1792, wrote:

The village of Gatehouse has thus been greatly enlarged within this short space of time by the addition of new streets and the extension of those which had been before begun. Its inhabitants are multiplied to the number of 1,500.[10]

In the nineteenth century, when steam replaced water as the main source of power, Gatehouse was too far from the coalfields to become a factory town. But industries nearer the mines in the Central Belt flourished.

Sinclair was a farmer, and neither he nor the majority of the ministers were as aware of the significance of industrial change as they were of changes in agriculture. But there were exceptions. Robert Douglas of Galashiels described in minute detail the processes involved in the manufacture of woollen cloth and concluded:

The manufacture of coarse woollen cloth is here carried on to a great extent. It has rapidly increased within these few years and is now brought to great perfection.[11]

He invested £1,000 of his own money in setting up a Cloth Hall which acted as an institute for improving technology. By mid-century Galashiels was producing fine cloth and had become the centre of the woollen industry in the Borders. Of the neighbouring parish of Peebles the Rev William Dalgleish wrote:

By the great increase of trade and opulence ... all classes are better educated, better lodged, better clothed and fed than in former times.[12]

More significant changes were taking place round the coalfields of the central belt. Mining had been an important industry since the thirteenth century; by the late eighteenth, steam-powered pumps made it possible to mine deeper and so to meet the demands of a rapidly growing industrial society. At Carron the most advanced technologies in metallurgy were being developed; in the west a fully mechanised cotton industry was employing thousands; in Leith and on Clydeside shipbuilding was becoming a major industry. The ministers in this region had no doubt about the significance of the changes. The Rev Robert Rennie of Kilsyth gave 20 pages to a description of the

9. Athelstaneford. An 'Improver's' village set in the fertile agricultural land of East Lothian.

industrial developments based on the mineral resources of his parish. John Wilson at Falkirk described the 'awful and sublime majesty' of the flashes of light from the ironworks at Carron and, watching traffic on the recently completed canal which was turning Grangemouth into a major port, wrote:

> A considerable part of those astonishing improvements which within these 40 years have been made in this parish has been owing to the great canal which is cut from the frith of Forth to the river Clyde.[13]

It was in this industrial belt that most of the engineers who emigrated to Poland had acquired their skills.

The south of Scotland was particularly hard hit by cyclical depressions after 1815. Sinclair believed that during the French Wars 'industry of other nations was checked and we commanded the markets of the universe'. In fact, overseas trade had often been erratic but home markets had been more stable. Scotland's factories had been producing coarse cloth for uniforms, canvas for sails and tents, leather for boots, and munitions for her own and her allies' armies. Farmers had enjoyed markets protected by Napoleon's Continental System which kept foreign grain out of British ports. Demand for corn and beef in the growing industrial towns, as well as in the armed forces, made farming profitable even on marginal land. By 1815 both foreign and home markets were collapsing and cheap corn flooded in from the Baltic states. Unemployment caused by enclosure of farm land and mechanisation of the textile industry was already serious; the discharge of servicemen made it worse. Deflation caused by return to the gold standard produced additional hardship. Thousands crowded into the industrial towns, prepared to work for any wage they could get.

In the 1790s the Rev Thomas Robertson of Dalmeny, near Edinburgh, had been able to write:

> A spirit of enterprise and for rising in the world characterizes the Scot in general: and this has so remarkably pervaded all ranks for these forty or fifty years past, that perhaps no people have in so short a period made such advances in industry, agriculture, manufactures, refinement and public revenue and private wealth as the people of Scotland.[14]

It was often amongst these achievers, if faced after 1815 with financial ruin and social disgrace, that the Polish landowners were to find the help they needed to transform their own impoverished estates. 'The opportunities in Scotland were not for those who had seen better days.'[15] To emigrate might seem the only alternative to poverty.

NOTES

1. R. Mitchison, *Agricultural Sir John*, 126.
2. K. L. Szyrma, *Reminiscences of a Journey through England and Scotland 1823–24* (unpublished translation).
3. *Ibid.*
4. *Statistical Account of Scotland*, vol. III, 561–2.
5. *Ibid*, vol. III, 682.
6. *Ibid*, vol. II, 637.
7. *Ibid*, vol. II, 445–6.
8. J. Sinclair, *Analysis of the Statistical Account of Scotland*, 273.

9. *Ibid*, 257.

10. I. Donnachie, in G. Cumming and T. M. Devine (eds), *Industry, Business and Society in Scotland since 1707*, 49.

11. *Statistical Account*, vol. III, 688.

12. *Ibid*, vol. II, 855.

13. *Ibid*, vol. IX.

14. *Ibid*, vol. II, 739.

15. R. H. Campbell, in R. A. Cage (ed.), *The Scots Abroad*, 15.

CHAPTER THREE

The Engineers

To William Coxe, a visiting Englishman, King Stanisław Poniatowski is reported to have said, 'Your house is raised, mine is yet to build'.[1] In the thirty years before the partitions he set out to do this. Poland was potentially a rich country. As part of the great European plain with a continental climate she was a major grain producer. From her forests she could export the timber needed by western maritime powers and her mineral resources included coal, iron, copper, silver, salt and lead. There were few barriers to communication. Nor, unfortunately, were there natural barriers to protect her riches. Wars in the seventeenth century with Sweden and Russia had devastated the country, and the stranglehold of the landowning classes on economic as well as political power had accelerated her decline. Danzig, a free port on the Baltic, was the only city represented in the parliament, the *sejm*. At a time when the Netherlands were enjoying a golden age under the leadership of an urban aristocracy, the burghers of Poland were deliberately stripped of the powers they had exercised in the Middle Ages. The Jewish community was used and abused but was politically powerless. To quote Zamoyski, 'The cities were so impoverished and legally ham-strung that no major enterprise could issue from them'.[2]

To regenerate the moribund economy Stanisław recognised that he would have to import foreign skills as well as foreign machines. Some of the most enlightened and powerful of the aristocracy had been doing this since the 1740s; by following their example Stanisław made 'improvement' fashionable. Linen manufacturers from Switzerland and silk workers from Lyons and Florence were invited to Poland to transfer their advanced technologies to craftsmen in his textile mills. Copper, silver, lead and salt mines were worked and marble was quarried. Antoni Tyzenhaus was appointed to develop royal estates in Lithuania and by 1780 the fifteen manufactories set up at Grodno employed over 1,500 people. Woollen and linen mills used raw materials produced on the king's estates but many of the new industries depended on imported materials, and catered for the luxuries for which the *szlachta*, the politically powerful landowners, had an apparently insatiable appetite – gold braid, tassels, carriages and silk sashes. Technical institutions were established to train Polish students, and an infrastructure of banks and roads was developed. Nearly 200 years after Timothy Pont's survey, on which the first accurate maps of Scotland were based, Hermann Perthees carried out the first geographical survey of Poland. This made the development of long-distance communications possible. When Frederick of Prussia imposed tariffs which strangled the old routes to the Baltic after the Partition of 1772, Polish rivers were linked to the Black Sea by the Ogiński and Royal canals. Polish boats could still take timber to the shipyards at Marseille and return with wine from Bordeaux. The Mediterranean route was shorter and probably safer than the traditional Baltic route. Trade with western Europe continued and between 1778 and 1788 exports rose by 500%.[3]

Tyzenhaus had called the manufactories and mines 'The diamonds in your crown' but, even before the partitioning powers had destroyed much of this achievement, many of the ventures had failed. The king and the magnates were enthusiastic amateurs:

> ... [they] had no understanding of markets, no grasp of long term investments, and no aptitude for the minutiae of business. Their ventures were usually inspired by foreign travel and suffered from all the characteristics of dilettantism. Factories were built up too fast and sums were not done. They would import foreign masters whose expertise they were in no position to verify.[4]

The Third Partition in 1795 terminated Stanisław's attempt to modernise his kingdom.

During the French Wars much of Poland had been a battleground and land went out of cultivation. When the Scottish agriculturalist, John Lumsden, visited Poland in 1813 he found many of the factories set up before 1793 in ruins. There was a complete absence of skilled craftsmen, and farmers were still using the most primitive of wooden implements. He attributed this to neglect by the magnates. They had lured technicians to Poland by promises which had not been kept, lost interest in projects which they had initiated and left the foreigners to the mercy of unscrupulous stewards who were opposed to change.

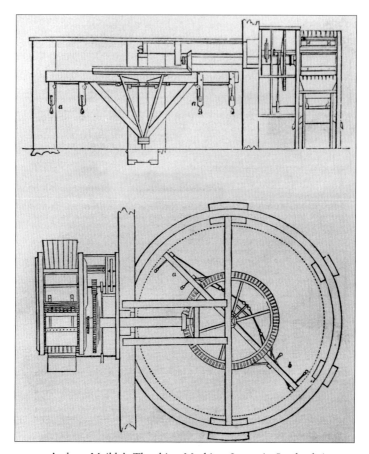

10. Andrew Meikle's Threshing Machine. In use in Scotland since
1786, threshing machines were the most important of the many
machines built by the Scots in Poland. From J. C. Loudon's *Encyclopedia
of Agriculture.*

But he noticed that some of the postwar landowners were of a different
calibre:

> The proprietors are now a different and very superior class of
> men to what they were 50 or 60 years ago. They have mostly
> been officers in the French army and with it have traversed the
> greater part of Europe.[5]

Count Ludwik Pac was one of the most outstanding of these younger
proprietors. The estates he inherited in north-east Poland and Lithuania

had been impoverished and depopulated during the wars. He had visited Britain before fighting as a general in Napoleon's armies and in 1814 made his second visit to Scotland. As a friend of Lord Brougham, he would have seen the achievements of improving landowners in the south of Scotland and the extent to which these depended on the use of sophisticated machinery and iron tools. On his own estates peasants were still using primitive wooden ploughs and threshing flails, and there were neither farmers capable of using modern machines nor mechanics able to make them. He deposited money in a Scottish bank to finance future purchases and returned to Poland with a set of models of the machines he had admired. The export of machinery from Britain was restricted till 1846, but parts and plans could be smuggled out. The next stage was to find engineers capable of reassembling the machines in Poland. Pac recruited the engineers and the models served as patterns for the implements which were to be made and used on his Dowspuda estate, near Białystok, before being given to the newly founded University of Warsaw.

Pac's companion during his first visit to Poland in 1803 had been Count Stanisław Zamoyski. There were nine towns and 291 villages on the family's 373,000-hectare estates in south-east Poland where the count was determined to introduce improved farming techniques. As a first step he brought back tradesmen to set up an agricultural machine factory at Zwierzynice near Zamość. These created what was probably the first significant colony of Scottish engineers and technicians to settle in Poland. The manager, from 1804 until his death in 1837, was John Macdonald, and two of his sons, John and Hector, were part of the team of smelters, blacksmiths, locksmiths, mechanics and turners who came out with him. Hector, 'millwright and engineer', was still working at Zamość in the 1840s. The tools and machines they made were some of those admired by neighbouring landowners who visited the Zamoyski model farms at Michałów and Greszczynka. Zwierzynice became the industrial centre of the Ordinacja, the administrative headquarters of the estates. There were brickworks, sawmills, engine works and a distillery. The brewery, founded in 1806 and equipped with machinery built by Macdonald's team, is still producing some of the best beer in Poland.

Amongst the engineers and technicians recruited in the west by

11. The Brewery, Zwierzyniec. Equipped with machinery built by John Macdonald, the Brewery was founded in 1806 and still produces some of the best beer in Poland.

Pac's agents in 1814 were more Scots. A report on 'The Situation on the Dowspuda Estate' dated March 1817 has survived and was recently discovered by the Polish historian Julian Bartyś.[6] It gives a very clear picture of what was happening. Scottish farmers and their families were arriving at Königsberg every spring. At a village still called 'Nowa Szkocja' Douglas and Robertson, 'good mechanics and engineers', were producing the machines essential for the advanced farming which the Scots had undertaken to introduce and for the industries related to agriculture which Pac intended to establish on his estate. The list is formidable: amongst others, fifteen different types of plough, two Meikle threshing machines, chaff cutters, an hydraulic press, seed drills, cranes and 'other machines used for easing manual labour'. For industry, they were building machines to be used in tanneries, breweries, distilleries and laundries. These were probably the machines displayed at exhibitions held in Warsaw in 1821 and 1823. All the work was reported to be of first quality and moulds were made from which copies could be taken. Although the engineers were foreign, the apprentices employed were Polish. This established a tradition which continued throughout the century, and was built into most later contracts between the government and foreign experts.

General Pac played a prominent part in the unsuccessful 1830 November Rising. When his estates were forfeited after its failure, management was handed over by their new owner, the Russian General Sulima, to an unscrupulous administrator who had no interest in agricultural or industrial innovations. All the industries collapsed.[7] Pac went into exile and many of the Scots moved south to the estate of the young Count Stanisław Zamoyski near Warsaw.

The fifteen years before the Rising had been a period of unprecedented growth when Czar Alexander I, as king of Poland, had encouraged its economic development. Although the Congress Kingdom was landlocked and western markets had been restricted since 1815 by Prussia's trade war against Poland, trade with Russia and the Far East had been opened up. The economy was under the guidance of Stanisław Staszic, head of the Department of Industry, and Prince Lubecki, a much travelled aristocrat who became head of the Treasury in 1821. He negotiated a treaty with the Russian government which opened the potentially enormous eastern market to Polish manufacturers. This, and long-term loans which were made available to improving landowners at 6% – a fraction of the rates normally charged by moneylenders – encouraged industrial development. In Warsaw a new university was founded and a preparatory school set up for a polytechnic which would have trained managers as well as scientists. Technical institutes were established at Marymont, for the study of agriculture and forestry, and at Kielce for mining. Many of the instructors were sent on prolonged tours of the main industrial countries of western Europe in order to gain experience of the most recent developments in technology. Universities and colleges laid the foundations for the emergence of a professional and skilled middle class.

For the first ten years, led by Lubecki, the initiative was usually taken by landowners; after 1828 the Bank Polski, and its vice-president, Prince Henryk Łubieński, played a more prominent part in promoting developments in industry. The Scottish Fergusson Tepper Bank, and many smaller banks founded in the eighteenth century, had been ruined by the Partitions and the exile of King Stanisław. To provide capital for new industries, Lubecki founded the Bank of Poland. In 1825 a government mission was sent to Britain to observe the latest technologies and recruit the personnel capable of transferring them to Poland. It included distinguished Poles like Stanisław Wysocki, Konstanty Wolicki and Wincenty Niepokejczycki, as well as the French inventor Philippe de Girard and the Welsh engineer Edward Thomas. Niepokejczycki's brief was to observe technical education in Britain but he also made a study of the Stockton to Darlington railway, the Edinburgh waterworks, Scottish farming and the organisation of joint-stock companies. Girard and Thomas looked for men and machines.[8] They bought parts and plans when they could and carried out industrial espionage where necessary. Lubecki had been impressed by the work of Scottish technicians when he had visited Charles Baird's munition factory near St Petersburg in 1811. David, one of Charles' sons, set up a successful engineering works at Lublin in 1817 but other Scots were recruited directly from Scotland. The postwar depressions in Britain made recruiting easier, as did special tax concessions and the free accommodation often provided for foreigners prepared to emigrate to Poland. Probably not more than 50 men were recruited, but they made a major contribution to the success of government economic policies by introducing new technologies and machinery. The growth of industry is reflected in trade figures; the deficit was reduced from seven million to one and a quarter million roubles between 1817 and 1830. Productivity increased dramatically in textiles, agriculture and the engineering works that serviced them.

The financing of the Evans Brothers' engineering works in Warsaw was one to which the Bank was to make a substantial contribution. In the 1820s these Welsh merchants had opened a shop which sold goods imported from Britain. By 1824 they were manufacturing the agricultural implements and industrial machinery previously imported and had persuaded Lubecki to provide credit and free accommodation for their factory. Built into their contract was an undertaking to train Polish mechanics, and when the Evans brothers retired in 1855, Stanisław Lilpop, a brilliant inventor trained by the Evans, became one of the directors. The Warsaw works survived the hostile trade policies introduced by Russia after the failure of the 1830 Rising. As Lilpop and Rau, it went over to heavy engineering and was still

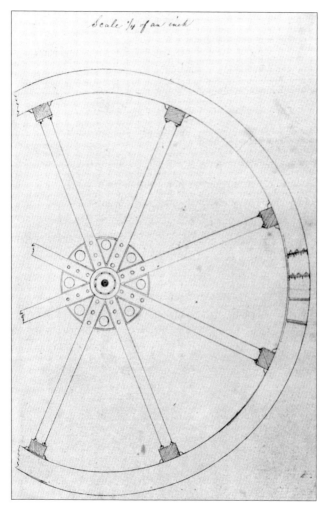

12. Section of a wheel. One of many diagrams in Kedslie's notebooks.

producing first-class machines at the end of the century. To quote the historian S. Niziol:

> The founding of these factories laid a firm foundation for a tradition of excellence in machine construction which was to be the main lasting legacy of British technology in the Kingdom.[9]

Some of the Scots were directly connected with the achievements of the Evans brothers. William Preacher, from Cavers in Roxburgh-shire, was probably enrolled by the Polish agents in Britain in 1825. He went out in 1826, worked with Evans, and was then contracted by the government to found the first state machine factory at Solec. This produced the steam engines essential for the modernisation of Polish industry. He was chief technical advisor at the Białogon factory near Kielce where he introduced modern British technologies. A team of ten immigrants there was assembling steam engines from imported parts and had the skill to build the flax-spinning and other machines which Girard was inventing for the linen factory at Żyrardów. Quoting a Polish historian, J. Szczepański writes: 'Thanks to Preacher, Białogon was able to provide for all the iron works belonging to the State'. These were the smelting and processing plants being built in Polish Silesia in the 1830s. In 1840 he was manager at Dąbrowa, where the Bank of Poland had the largest steelworks in Europe, and a few years later was head of a private firm near Lublin. He was an inventor of distinction, and in 1833 and 1839 visited France and Britain in order to recruit personnel and keep in touch with industrial developments in the West.[10] At a time when a Scottish puddler employed in Poland was being paid 3,360 złoty a year, Preacher's salary was 9,000 złoty. When he died in Warsaw in 1858, he left his wife Agnes Bell a wealthy woman.

Preacher was the most distinguished of the Scottish engineers of his time in Poland. Less well known was George Irvine, born in Glasgow in 1800 and a manager of the Evans factory at Kuznica Drzewicka. A Polish contemporary described him as

> ... able and knowledgeable ... a man well educated in respect to his occupation and is familiar with innovations and under-standing of fundamentals ... dedicated to his work.[11]

Another was John Crowe, head of a group of British mechanics at Nietulisko. His son Edward, who was born in Poland in 1830, became a civil engineer in Warsaw and married a daughter of Henry Marconi, one of the distinguished Italian architects who had worked for General Pac. George Blaikie, an expert in the manufacture of threshing machines, had also started his career in Poland at Dowspuda. With a salary of 2,000 złoty, a house, garden, farm produce and fuel he must

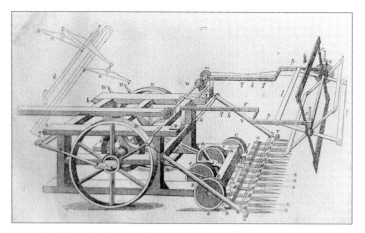

13. Patrick Bell's Reaper. Invented in Angus in 1826, the reaper was almost as great a labour saver as the threshing machine.

have been relatively well off. He befriended William Hay and probably other emigrants on their arrival at Nowa Szkocja. By the 1830s he had moved to the Zamoyski estate and then to Austrian Galicia, still making threshing machines for Polish landowners there. As major labour savers, these were the most popular of all the agricultural machines introduced in the nineteenth century. By 1860 there were probably 12,000 in use on Polish estates. Blaikie worked on his own; Charles Macleod managed a factory at Skąpe which specialised in the development of an improved American plough. In the consular records he appears as having died young, in debt and without a will but his son Alexander was able to set up his own machine factory and by 1870 was able to buy an estate. He was one of the first of the Scots to be polonised. He married a Pole and the name became Machlejd. In 1938 a Machlejd, probably one of his descendants, visited my parents in Leeds. My mother helped him to re-establish links with Dunvegan and the Macleods.

The Douglas family was one of the many whose members were all in the south by the 1830s. Of the three brothers, Andrew was managing a brewery at Lublin, Hector was an engineer who was in charge of the Białogon works during Preacher's absence in 1838–39, and John was manager of a papermill for Prince Czartoryski at Celejów. His partner Andrew Kedslie was another Borderer and another of my ancestors. The dimensions of the chaff-cutting, washing and beating machines at the papermill, and of the waterwheel which powered them, are carefully recorded in his cousin Alexander Kedslie's note-book. By the time of the Rising the partners owned the mill and in 1834 they set up their own engineering factory. Their contract with the Bank Polski has survived. This was for a new venture in Lublin. They had to organise, within a year, a factory for the production of agricultural machinery and tools and had to keep it going for ten years. The Bank had to provide credit of 20,000 złoty and mining firms were to provide the different types of metal they would need. A six-horsepower steam engine and a lathe were to be supplied on credit from the Solec factory and tools could be ordered from Białogon. Repayment at 6% was to begin in 1836 and to be completed in eight years. The state was to secure repayment and could seize the factory and personal property to do so.[12] Douglas and Kedslie were reputed to be excellent mechanics but poor businessmen. When the factory closed in 1839 they were producing good machines and had full order books but no money with which to pay the workers. Both men died in debt. Kedslie was still paying off the last instalments when employed as a clerk on the Vienna railway in the 1880s.

There were few ventures that did not fail during the bleak years between the 1830 Rising and the Crimean War in 1853. The Russian viceroy, Paskievich, set out to halt the industrial development of Poland as well as to destroy such political independence as had survived after Nicholas I came to the throne in 1825. Pac was accompanied into exile by Lubecki, Czartoryski, Wolicki and thousands of the most enterprising of the upper classes who had provided capital and support for foreign experts. Russian markets and, through Russia, Far Eastern outlets were closed and the domestic market was too small to sustain industrial growth. Łubieński remained as vice-president of the Bank Polski but by 1842 he and the president, Lubowidzki, were on trial, accused of mismanagement and corruption. The credit squeeze which followed this scandal, 'the affair Łubieński', destroyed most ventures which depended on the Bank for finance. Even Preacher's private factory failed and the Żyrardów linen firm only just survived the years when its management was in the hands of the Bank. Niziol describes Poland in the years after the Rising as 'a small economy with a poorly developed internal market, politically dependent on a state that was hostile to any economic progress'. Recovery had to wait till 'The Thaw' which followed the accession of Alexander II in 1855. The Russian government was then shocked by its failure in the Crimean War into measures to build up the industrial potential of the Empire. The Scots had made a substantial contribution to the development of the economy but were caught up in the Polish tragedy. The children of those who stayed on were to build on the foundations laid by their fathers.

NOTES

1. A. Zamoyski, *The Last King of Poland*, 239.
2. *Ibid*, 244.
3. *Ibid*, 252.
4. *Ibid*, 244.
5. J. C. Loudon, *Encyclopaedia of Agriculture*, 104.
6. J. Bartyś, *English and Scottish Farmers in Poland*, 99.
7. S. Niziol, *British Technology and Polish Development*, 7.
8. *Ibid*, 40.
9. *Ibid*, 42.
10. J. Szczepański, *Modernizacja Gornictwa i Hutnictwa w Królestwie Polskim XIX*, 234.
11. *Ibid*, 243.
12. H. Radziszewski, *Bank Polski*, 253.

CHAPTER FOUR

The Metallurgists

Like Polish engineers in the nineteenth century, Scots in the early eighteenth were largely dependant on iron smelted in small furnaces. These were often in the Highlands, where charcoal could be produced cheaply in northern woods. In 1753 the Carron Company was founded by the Yorkshireman Dr Roebuck to set up the first foundry in Scotland designed to smelt with coke, using coal and iron ore from the Central Belt. The start was disastrous. In 1766 James Watt built his first improved steam engine at Carron, but to find the precise workmanship necessary to perfect the design he had to move to Birmingham. Although skilled gun founders had been brought up from England, the cannons supplied to the Board of Ordnance acquired such a reputation for bursting that, in 1773, they were withdrawn from naval vessels. But within a few years many of the technical problems experienced during the company's early days had been solved. The short-barrelled cannon, the carronade, became the most reliable gun available for naval warfare, and by the 1780s cannons were being exported to Russia, the Netherlands, Portugal and Spain. Mr James Wilson, the minister at Falkirk, believed that by the 1790s nearly 2,000 men were employed in connection with the works, whose 'flashes of light ... appear in awful and sublime majesty'. From the start there had been four blast furnaces, sixteen air and three cupola furnaces. Water was the main source of power; the only steam engine installed was used to recirculate water from the eighteen wheels. The company owned its own coal and ironstone mines and, as production soared, increasingly imported high-quality ores from Sweden through the new port at Grangemouth. Clydeside foundries were to develop in the same way and by 1790 the Forth and Clyde canal linked the two areas. As Mr Wilson reported:

A considerable part of those astonishing improvements which within these forty years, have been made in this parish, has been owing to the great canal, which is cut from the frith of Forth to the river Clyde.[1]

It was often at Carron that the men who took the new technologies to eastern Europe had learned their skills. Charles Gascoigne, the Company's director from 1769–86, emigrated to Russia, taking machinery and a team of skilled workers with him. The techniques they

14. Prince Henry Łubieński. Łubieński was vice-president of the Bank Polski which initiated and financed much of the metallurgical industry in Silesia in the 1830s. He also played an important role in the establishment of the linen industry in Żyrardów.

15. Baird's Works, St Petersburg. Charles Baird had been head of the casting and finishing department at Carron before he went out to Russia. The quality of the work produced by Scottish engineers and mechanics in Baird's and other factories in Russia in the early nineteenth century encouraged Lubecki to recruit skilled men from Scotland.

introduced revolutionised the Russian armaments industry. He was followed by Charles Baird, whose St Petersburg foundry Lubecki had admired, while in Prussian Silesia, John Baildon, another engineer from Carron, was introducing similar technologies. Staszic, who was responsible for economic development in Poland from 1815–30, had visited Gliwice in 1805 to inspect Baildon's blast furnaces but he made no attempt to import the new techniques to Poland. He was more interested in opening up iron, silver and lead mines than in developments in metallurgy. Much of the pig-iron used by Charles Baird's son David and other Scots working in Polish factories was smelted in small charcoal-fired furnaces whose design had changed little since the Middle Ages. Water power was introduced to drive the bellows but it was the 1830s before the first blast furnace was built in Poland.

During the Paskievich period, when Poland was put under military rule after the failure of the 1830 Rising, the Bank Polski was responsible for mining and metallurgy. There were considerable deposits of ironstone around Kielce, in Staropolskie in the south-east, and of coal around Dąbrowa, in Polish Silesia in the south-west. But they were 200 kilometres apart and it was 1859 before a rail link was created between the coalfields of the Dąbrowa Basin and the rest of Poland. In spite of this, the directors of the Bank decided to develop a massive metallurgical industry in Silesia. Ironstone was to be smelted in coke-fired furnaces and refined and processed by the most advanced British and German techniques. French and Polish experts assured the directors that coal from the Dąbrowa Basin was suitable for coking, and smelting capacity was planned to provide iron for a railway system which would link industrial Poland with European and eastern markets. As early as 1838 the quality of the coal and the proposed capacity of the ironworks were being questioned by the British consul and the business community in Warsaw but the Bank went ahead with its plans. Enormous sums were invested and foreign experts recruited. Eight blast furnaces and supporting refining and processing plants were built. Those at Dąbrowa were intermittently in production by the 1840s; the works at Niwka were never fully operative and were closed permanently in 1842.

The enterprise was a disastrous failure. Dąbrowa coal produced such poor coke that iron smelted in the new furnaces was brittle; no amount of processing and refining could make it fit for use. Charcoal-smelted iron had to be carted the 200 kilometres from the Kielce region to Dąbrowa to keep the puddling and finishing plants in production. The railway project, for which iron production had been planned, was launched on the London stock market in 1839. But the prospectus was fraudulent. Costs – and profits – had been calculated on the assumption that trains would be horse-drawn. The decision to use

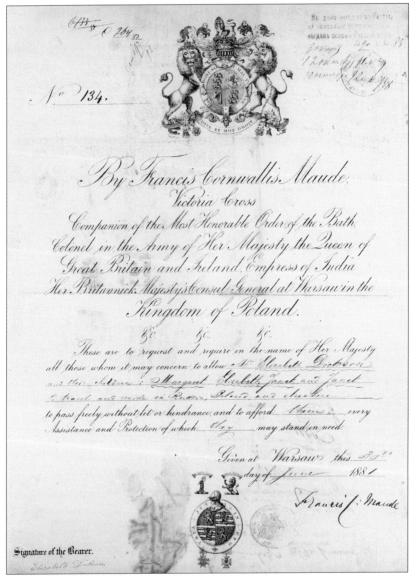

16.   Passports. The engineer Alexander Watson complained that he had had to surrender his passport when he arrived in Poland in 1834. The consul in Warsaw issued passports to British citizens born in Poland. Elizabeth Dickson's, dated 1881, is the earliest of my mother's family's to have survived. Although she lived in Poland till 1906, she was described as 'of Edinburgh' when her second one was issued by the Lord Provost of Edinburgh in 1896. A British passport saved one of her grand-daughters from a Nazi gas chamber in 1941.

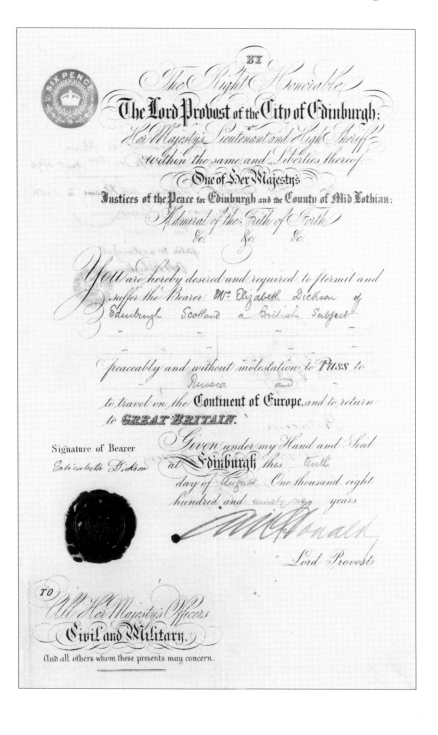

steam power was not made till 1840 and raised projected costs from 21 to 38 million złoty. By 1842 the project had been abandoned.[2] Only the line from Warsaw to Vienna was built. This made troop movements easier for the Russian army but industrial regions were bypassed. Coal from Dąbrowa still had to be transported on horse-drawn carts and its price trebled before it reached Warsaw. When the railways were at last developed after the Crimean War, rails had to be imported from Wales. British pig-iron was still cheaper and better than iron produced in Poland. Production, which rose 200% between 1830 and 1840, plummeted and did not recover the 1840 level till the Dąbrowa works were reorganised under new owners in 1876. Till then they had never operated at more than 40% capacity.[3]

What part did the Scots play in this sorry story? William Preacher was directly involved, supplying furnaces, cranes and rolling mills from the Białogon factory and overseeing installation at Huta Ban-kowa, the Bank Polski's ironworks. William Macconnel, who joined Preacher in 1827, was repairing furnaces for the Huta in the 1840s and John Crowe was in charge of a group of British technicians who had been recruited to train Polish workers at Netulisko.[4] The most significant figure was Alexander Watson. His family had owned land at Priestfield, near Edinburgh, and the younger sons had been emigrating to the Baltic countries since the seventeenth century. Alexander's brother Thomas was farming on the Dowspuda estate in 1825 and probably persuaded him to come out to Poland. Alexander joined him in the early 1830s and was appointed by the Bank Polski to be engineer in charge of factories and foundries in Silesia. He was an expert on steam power and introduced into Poland Neilson's hot-blast process. This had been developed in Scotland and patented in 1828. Using heated air to fan the furnaces, it reduced the quantity and halved the cost of fuel necessary for smelting. In 1839 he was moved by the Bank from smelting to mining. He was living on the frontier and, in a letter to the British consul in July 1840, complained of restrictions placed on his movements by the Russian government. He had understood that the visa issued to him by the Russian consul in Leith in 1833 would be valid for an unlimited period, but on his arrival in Warsaw this had had to be surrendered. Since then per-mission to stay in Dąbrowa had been issued annually but the latest permit had been for only six months. He appealed to the consul for a more general passport:

> I would most respectfully beg leave to enquire of your Excellency if it would not be possible when I am getting a new Passport to get a more general one not alone to Poland but through Poland to Prussia, Cracow [still a free state], Austria etc, and this to a British Subject I think the Russian government would not object to, although they do not allow it to a born Pole, but not for once only but for crossing the frontiers as often as may be necessary; as we are here, though living on the very borders of these countries, completely cut off from all communication with them; I have friends and acquaintances there, and I might, had I a free Passport, often see new Works which might be servicable to me in my profession.[5]

He signed himself 'Engineer to the Bank of Poland'. The private metallurgical factory he set up with Polish partners was unsuccessful and in 1846 he planned to move to Galicia. In a letter to the consul he wrote: 'Besides this the service is now attended with so many unpleasantries which I, as a foreigner, ... [am] at liberty to leave them at any time'. He died a few months later and by the 1860s his widow Agnes Kedslie had returned to Scotland.

Until recently Polish historians have been severely critical of the foreigners employed by the Bank in its development of the metallurgical industry – 'charlatans unemployable anywhere else in Europe'. There were some rogues amongst the 50 or so British recruited and probably a degree of nepotism. The Protestant foreign community, French, Italian and German as well as English, Welsh and Scots, became increasingly closely knit by marriage. During the promising years of the Congress Kingdom, the Scots had encouraged relatives to emigrate and did what they could to find them salaried jobs. Alexander Watson is an example. He had married Agnes Kedslie before he left Scotland. Her cousin Andrew had emigrated in the early 1820s; her brother Alexander in 1829. The family network was close on her side as well as Watson's. Kedslie's notebooks suggest that contact was maintained between the engineers and metallurgists. He made innumerable entries related to crucibles, moulds, pyrometers etc and to the relative costs and qualities of fuels available for smelting and steam power. A typical entry reads:

To convert cubic foot of water into steam
Newcastle and coking coal	8.40 lbs
Coke	7.70 lbs
Charcoal	10.60 lbs [6]

Surviving records suggest a high degree of responsibility amongst many of the Scots; perhaps the less responsible left fewer records.

After 1830 conditions deteriorated drastically, but the Bank offered high salaries and attractive contracts to foreign employees. At a time when Polish smiths were earning 360 złoty a year, German technicians were paid 1,500 złoty and British puddlers 3,360. For every Pole they trained there was a bonus of 120 złoty. Housing for Polish workers was estimated to cost 1,200 złoty; houses for the British could cost as much as 7,000 złoty. In some of the contracts free fuel and housing were promised as well as the cost of repatriation if the two-year contract were not renewed. And for six years the foreigners lived tax-free.[7] High wages may have attracted some unsatisfactory workers, but there is no evidence to suggest that the Scots failed in their role as conveyors of sophisticated technologies. That the technologies were inappropriate to the Polish economy was the fault of the Bank's advisors and not of the foreign experts it recruited. Its president and vice-president, Lubowidzki and Łubieński, were arrested on charges of corruption in 1842. If not corrupt, they were, to quote Niziol, certainly responsible for 'a system of extravagance, peculation and mismanagement' and for 'puddlers with nothing to puddle and rolling mills with nothing to roll'.[8]

The problems faced by British settlers in Poland in the 1830s and 1840s are well documented in the consular records. They go some way to explain why high salaries had to be offered to persuade foreigners to come to Poland. Damage to their property during the Rising was so serious that in December 1831 a delegation headed by one of the Evans brothers persuaded the Foreign Minister, Lord Palmerston, to send out a consul. One of the first men to hold this position, Colonel Barnett, travelled extensively in Poland and was a shrewd observer. By 1838 he was asking the Foreign Office to discourage would-be emigrants from coming to Poland. He was talking about 'Englishmen' but his comments were probably relevant to at least some of the Scots. To Lord Palmerston he wrote:

> I may be allowed to offer a few remarks on the evils resulting from the practice which exists to a considerable extent of engaging workmen in England to go out to that country. They are induced by the offer of high wages to leave their homes, often with their wives and families. On their arrival in Poland they are met with many difficulties and petty vexations from the Local Authorities in regard to their passports and the admission of their few effects. The undertakings for which they are engaged nine times out of ten fail and the men being then no longer of any use turn adrift. I have myself been witness to the ill treatment which at such periods they receive from those who had engaged them to come out ... It may be a matter of consideration for Her Majesty's Government whether some measures may not be taken for putting Workmen in the Manufacturing districts of England on their guard against being induced to go out to Poland by the prospect held out of getting better wages and constant employment.[9]

Barnett was referring to workmen who have left few marks on Polish economic history but his records are full of complaints from substantial Scots whose property had been damaged or who were suffering from the corruption of Russian officials and the lawlessness of the army and police. In 1834 James Garvie claimed successfully for 259.67 roubles owed to him as salary by Prince Ogińsky but failed to get compensation for damage to his 'manufactury'.[10] In 1837 Alexander Douglas was complaining about a fourteen-month delay in the extension of his permission to stay in Lublin where he had set up a brewery two years before 'for the manufacture of porter and ale by the English system'.[11] The case of Alexander Kedslie is worth quoting as an example of the kind of harassment to which British citizens were being subjected. Kedslie, an engineer and miller from Edinburgh, had come out in 1829 to manage the Warsaw steam mill for Prince Potocki. In 1835 he rented Rosancie, a farm on the Zamoyski estate on the border of Austrian Galicia. In June 1838, writing from Warsaw, he complained to the consul about the seizure of his papers by officials who refused to show any authorisation for their action. 'I consider it my duty to myself and Country to lay the following facts before you', he wrote. He had been charged with holding a correspondence with people in Austria, the implication being that he was involved in smuggling. He described his only connection with Austria, a letter about the issue of a passport to a former employee who had moved to Galicia, and continued:

> I conceive it is no difficult matter to find out the reasons why my papers were seized. Having determined from my first settlement in Rosancie to have nothing to do with smuggling I did not consider it necessary to court the favour of the straznics [border guards] belonging to the village. They have even without leave asked turned their horses on my meadows and clover fields, the consequence was I caught their horses repeatedly but gave them up without exacting any damage from them. At last their insolence was such that one of them came with his sabre drawn and took his horse out of my stable and threatened one of my sons that if any person laid hold on his horse he would strike him with his sword and that he would pasture his horse upon my wheat fields if he happened to be near them when on patrol. In such a situation I complained to the head of the strazniks at Tarnogrod who promised to write the person complained of which, if he did, it would seem it had no effect as their horses were seen pasturing on my ground two days before I left home.
>
> Having given you this simple statement I have you to act in my case as you deem proper and can only repeat that I do not believe there was ever one of my countrymen who has ever done less than I have either in word or act to render him liable to suspicion to the Imperial Government for I have ever held it as a rule that a foreigner has no right to intermeddle with the affairs of any country in which he may choose to take up his residence and that if he is not satisfied his best way is to leave it.[12]

Barnett took up the complaint with the Russian government, referring to Kedslie as 'to my knowledge a person of unexceptionable character', and adding:

I cannot refrain from remarking that the arbitrary behaviour of the local authorities on this occasion appears in this case to merit the severe censure of the government.[13]

Chipoff, the Russian official who replied to the consul's protest, dismissed the incident as being unimportant and due to a misunderstanding. There is no reference to the behaviour of the mounted guards or to the local authorities.[14] In a letter to his grandson Thomas Garvie, at school in Edinburgh thirty years later, Kedslie wrote:

> Dear as you are to me and much as I miss you in my now lonely room I rejoice for the sake of your future welfare that you have left this miserable country and you are placed where you will enjoy advantages both as regard your future prospects in life and above all those which regard a future and eternal state ...[15]

Of the development of the metallurgical industry Niziol wrote:

> There were no major and few provincial plants where the British were not involved in positions of authority ... [but] the Kingdom could offer little in the way of political stability and personal security for the crucial period of the Paskievich regime.[16]

However successfully they may have transferred technologies, their experiences during the 1830s and 1840s must have made many of them, like Kedslie, wish that they had never left home. When the Dąbrowa works were restructured in 1876, capital and initiative came from France; British input during the second half of the nineteenth century appears to have been negligible.

NOTES

1. J. Sinclair (ed.), *Statistical Account*, Vol. IX, 304.
2. S. Niziol, *British Technology and Polish Economic Development*, 60.
3. *Ibid*, 57.
4. J. Szczepański, *Modernizacja Gornictwa i Hutnictwa w Królestwie Polskim w i Połowie*, XIX W, 240.
5. Foreign Office Consular Records, 392/1 100.
6. A. Kedslie, Notebooks.
7. S. Niziol, *op cit.*, 43.
8. *Ibid*, 35.
9. *Ibid*, 45.

10. Foreign Office, 393/2.
11. Foreign Office, 392/1 57.
12. *Ibid*, 84.
13. *Ibid*, 90.
14. Foreign Office, 393/2 40.
15. Garvie Letters (unpublished), 1864–72.
16. S. Niziol, *op cit.*, 52.

CHAPTER FIVE

The Farmers

Engineers like John Macdonald went out to Poland at the start of the nineteenth century to build the agricultural machines essential for improved farming. For his patron, Count Stanisław Zamoyski, the next step was to import farmers capable of using them effectively. Germans were believed to be practising advanced farming methods but the settlement of Rhineland farmers on his estates in the south-east was a failure. The Polish historian Julian Bartyś quotes a contemporary report:

> The settlers in Sitaniec like others of the same kind give themselves up to the habit of excessive drinking. This vice is so widespread that in spite of the favourable conditions of their colonies they are not at all well off financially ... they have not started a single elementary school until now and the majority cannot read or write. In general they have made no progress but rather regressed.[1]

Near Suwałki in the north-east, on his Raczki and Dowspuda estates, General Pac's experience was similar: after a year he was clearing the Germans off the land on which he had invited them to settle. In 1814 he returned to Scotland, determined to replace them with some of the farmers whose skills he had so admired on an earlier visit.

How backward was Polish farming? During his 1813–14 European tour, J. C. Louden spent several months near Warsaw and wrote:

> Poland was formerly the granary of Europe ... At present its boundaries are so circumscribed and its arable surface so indifferently cultivated ... that it furnishes little more corn than supplies its own population.[2]

King Stanisław and a few of his more enlightened nobles had introduced modern methods on their estates in the late eighteenth century, but Louden noted that almost all the enterprises initiated before the Partitions had been abandoned. As has so often happened,

Poland had become a battleground during the Napoleonic Wars and land had gone out of cultivation. What was left of the corn trade was wrecked by the French blockade of the Baltic ports.

Louden recognised one of the problems:

> The landed estates are almost everywhere large. Estates are farmed by the proprietors by means of stewards ... There are scarcely any rent paying farmers.[3]

It was a largely illiterate peasantry that worked the land. Although serfdom had been abolished in 1791, it could be legally reimposed after the 1815 settlement. Many serfs were given personal freedom by their owners, but rent for land was usually paid in kind and by services. This, the *corvée*, was normally two days' labour a week on the landowners' farms. With three-year leases, they farmed their own strips of arable land and grazed a few stunted animals on village meadows and heaths. These were neither drained nor cultivated. From a third to half the land lay fallow and fodder crops and crop rotations were almost unknown. Estates were windswept and unenclosed and stewards were often as suspicious of change as the most ignorant serf. When General Chłapowski tried to introduce Scottish farming on his Turew estate on the frontiers of western Poland, his officials decided that he had gone mad and resigned.[4] If productivity were to be increased, proprietors were going to have to persuade educated and experienced farmers to lease land on their estates.

The postwar depression in Britain played into their hands. In 1822 Louden wrote about Scottish farming:

> Agriculture has sustained a severe shock from the fall in prices ... [there is] a picture of widely spread ruin among the agricultural classes ... In the shock many of the farmers lost all their capital and were obliged to become operatives for others: while some, more fortunate, were able to retain enough of their property as enabled them to emigrate to other countries.[5]

William Hay was one of the more fortunate ones. Descended from minor landowners in Aberdeenshire, his maternal grandfather, the Rev. Robert Douglas of Galashiels, was the author of *A General View of the Agriculture of Roxburgh and Selkirk* and a driving force behind the

17. Dowspuda, *c.* 1850. The neo-Gothic house, built for General Pac by the Italian architects Charles and Henry Marconi, was at the centre of the estate on which 500 Scots are believed to have settled between 1815 and 1830.

development of the textile industry in the Borders. His father, the Rev. James Hay, was minister of the nearby parish of Roberton. In a surviving testimonial, written in Latin and dated February 4th 1819, he commended William to General Pac and described the training his son had had in both Scottish and English farming methods.[6] In a letter to his son in 1824 Hay wrote:

> I am glad you find yourself comfortable and have the prospect of becoming more so ... Our farmers have not, almost since you left, been able to pay the rents and have generally been allowed an abatement.[7]

William was something of a ne'er-do-weel, marrying 'beneath him', seldom answering letters and swallowing up a legacy intended for the benefit of his children. But he was only one amongst about sixty farmers persuaded by Pac and his agents to emigrate between 1815 and 1830. The Dowspuda estate was on the borders of Lithuania, and, through the port of Königsberg, was easily reached from Leith. Many of these men, including William's son James, were first-rate farmers. I know the detailed background only of those who, like the Hays, were related to my mother. They all came from the Lowlands, were of landowning stock and were in financial difficulties at home. The exception were the Govenlocks whom my mother was convinced had gipsy blood; clearly not gentlefolk, they came out as skilled ploughmen and became very successful farmers. Land was cheap by Scottish standards. Describing the building of a new farm steading near Edinburgh in 1834, William Hay's sister Beatrix wrote: 'The Farm Offices were to cost seven hundred pounds. With you the sum would have bought a handsome estate'. A few of the Scots did buy farms and estates but most started by renting on long leases. Other familiar Lowland names are in the record: Thompson, Riad [Riach?], Burns, Shiels, Robertson, Garvie, Watson, Dobbie, and Broomfield. Most had single tenancies but both Walter Govenlock and John Dickson, and George and Andrew Broomfield, started by farming as partners.

Some of these leases have survived in the National Archives at Suwałki, translated into English by John Lomany, Pac's secretary, and Peter Stuart, one of his stewards.[8] The statement which preceded their signatures – 'I recognise the aforesaid tenants and also attest that this is a true translation from the Polish lease' – suggests that they had been the recruiting agents in Scotland. Leases were for 25 years and ensured that the Scots would improve the Dowspuda estate, as their grandparents had improved many a barren acre in Scotland. On farms of from 176 to 353 acres, they were to fence, hedge, ditch and drain their land, all materials being provided by the proprietor. Turnips, clover and potatoes were to be introduced into four- and six-year rotations. There would be two rent-free years and six free of government taxes. When the British Corn Laws led to a slump in the price of Baltic wheat, Pac decreased some of the rents by about 10%. In 1821 he modified the lease, signed by William Burn in 1817, with the preface:

> His Excellency the Proprietor having a regard on the present hard times and wishing to encourage the farmers to further advances and endeavours resolved to make the following diminution and alteration in the payment on the farm rent agreed on by the contract made 23 of April 1817.

Half his estate was let to Scots. Peasants who were cleared off land

18. Clydesdale Stallion. Powerful horses were essential for the mechanisation of farming. Polish landowners and the farmers on their estates were importing breeding stock directly from Britain.

which they had previously farmed as part of a village community became landless labourers. Villages like Korytki and Wielka Pruska became enclosed farms and names like Linton, Berwick or Broomfield appeared on estate maps. Work was done by the farmer and his family and by Polish employees. Where necessary, materials were provided to build a farmhouse, steading and cottages. At Nowa Szkocja a colony of foreigners settled. Amongst these were George Blaikie, the thresh-ing-machine expert, and John Heiton, the gardener from Selkirk who created the gardens around Dowspuda. His daughter Margaret married Charles Marconi, one of the Italian architects who designed the Gothic Revival palace and many other buildings on the Pac estate. Unfortun-ately, none of the farm buildings has survived and the palace, clearly inspired by the Romantic movement and with crockets that remind one of Roslin Chapel in Midlothian, is a ruin. His second daughter, Alice, married George Broomfield, one of the farmers who later moved to the Zamoyski estates. These Protestant foreigners became so closely intermarried that my mother was related to most of them.

When General Pac died in exile, a few years after the failure of the

1830 Rising, he mentioned the Scottish farmers in his will but their joint achievements were never publicised. The Agricultural Society which Pac and Zamoyski founded in 1815 was short-lived. There were several exhibitions of agricultural machinery in Warsaw in the 1820s but no equivalents in Poland of the Holkham 'sheep-shearings' or Lothian agricultural shows until 1843.

Two very early reports 'On the situation on the Dowspuda estate' have, however, survived and are quoted by Julian Bartyś.[9] In 1817 an unidentified author wrote that by 1816 Robert Thompson, the steward at Nova Szkocja, was importing pure-bred bulls and merino sheep. He had planted 56 acres of turnips, 56 of potatoes:

> On a well manured, well cultivated field that had been cleared of couch grass he sowed 121 acres of wheat where, in consequence of the abandonment of the farmstead and of the neglected cultivation, only 75 acres had been sown before.[10]

The second report was made in 1821. The observer noted that many of the Scots were well off and inspected farms carefully before signing a lease. They then cleaned land by deep ploughing and drilling and built up fertility with manure before introducing clover and turnips. Of the farmers he wrote:

> The customs and habits of Scots are blameless. They like Polish vodka but mix it with beer, water or other fluids. They are very thrifty and while in fields work harder than locals. They mix farm manure with peat ... they complain that they cannot get lime ... Very diligently they make hay, cutting grass wherever they can find it. They might be short of capital to buy more cattle as they sell some of the hay. However, the most extraordinary thing is that although they carry out most ordinary farm work, everyone can read and write and count. Some of them have a collection of these books and sometimes they read them.

Some of these books came back with Thomas Garvie in 1906: the family Bibles of the Dicksons and the Govenlocks and Alexander Kedslie's copy of Louden's *Encyclopaedia of Agriculture*. John Dickson took out his mother Janet's copy of Bishop Burnett's *History of My Own Time*, inscribed 'To my dear cousin J. Burnett from the author'.

19. The Scotch Cart. This could be pulled by one good horse and was light, versatile and efficient. From J. C. Loudon.

The author was the distinguished seventeenth-century cleric who had been tutor to 'The Patriot', Andrew Fletcher of Saltoun, and later became bishop of Salisbury. Janet had been impoverished by the death of her husband and loss of his land in America during the War of Independence. Her father's family had given her a cottage on the Barnes estate but she was too poor to educate her children. John Dickson was described not as a farmer but as 'an honest ploughman' when he emigrated. Like most of the Scots he moved south after the 1830 Rising. Under its new Russian owner conditions at Dowspuda seem to have become intolerable.

Desydery Chłapowski, like Pac a former general in Napoleon's army, was another admirer of Scottish agriculture. At the end of the wars he returned to an estate at Turew, near Poznań, which was unproductive and heavily mortgaged. Visits to Britain in 1814 and 1818 convinced him that productivity could be raised by the introduction of both machines and new farming techniques. During a prolonged visit to George Rennie's model farm, Phantassie, at East Linton in the Lothians, he was taught how to build corn and haystacks and how to handle James Small's swing ploughs. Invented in the 1760s by a Berwickshire smith, their curved iron mouldboards had revolutionised the cultivation of arable land. Soil could be deepened, weeds controlled and sophisticated machinery used on well-worked land. Rennie, the son of a tenant farmer, had himself been sent to study the work of improvers in the Tweed valley before taking over his father's tenancy at Phantassie in the 1760s. When he died in 1828, his achievements were engraved on his headstone:

> In this country so celebrated for its fertile soil and the perfection of its cultivation Mr Rennie was aknowledged by his contemporaries to be the most skilful and successful agriculturalist. Nor was the reputation he so justly merited confined to his native land. He corresponded with and [was] visited not only by the leading agriculturalists of England and Ireland but many noblemen and gentlemen from France, Russia, Germany, Poland and Hungary and other European states seeking information to improve their domains were hospitably received by him and instructed in his theories and practices.

Rennie's was an example that Chłapowski decided to follow, and his experiments and achievements were recorded in his *O Rolnitcwie* and other agricultural journals. He believed that 'to deepen one's soil is equal to buying a second farm' [11] but his land was farmed by peasants who were as unwilling as his stewards to adopt new methods or use a swing plough. They preferred the home-made implements described by Louden:

> We have seen lands ploughed (after their manner) by one cow, tied by the horns to the trunk of a young fir tree, one of the roots sharpened as a share and the other serving the ploughman as a handle. In other instances we have seen a pair of oxen pulling a wretched implement formed by the peasant who is in all cases his own plough and wheel wright as well as house carpenter and builder. Their best or usual plough has no mould board.[12]

In sandy soil this might break up the surface, but would leave the land infested with weeds and too rough to make the use of drills or reapers possible. It was only after he had replaced his stewards and peasants with educated farmers on long improving leases that progress was possible. With their help he paid off debts of a million złoty and, by 1830, the value of his estate increased by one and a quarter million. At his own expense, and at a time when the Russian government was

20. The Manager's House, Michalów, 1997. Under Andrew Kedslie's management at Michalów, Andrzej Zamoyski was proving in the 1840s that Scottish farming practices could be adapted successfully to Polish conditions.

closing down universities and training colleges, he set up a school in which 150 young Poles were trained in the practice as well as the theory of Scottish farming. Although his estates were in what had become Prussian Poland, his influence was significant in the Congress Kingdom.[13]

By mid-century the Zamoyski family was playing a crucial role in raising the standard of farming. Its vast estates in south-east and central Poland were being provided with machinery from the factory at Zwierzyniec which John Macdonald had been managing since 1803. In 1820 Count Stanisław sent his sons to look at estate management in Britain. From Holkham Hall in Norfolk, where Count Andrzej attended the last of the great sheep-shearing demonstrations, they went to Edinburgh University to study economics and farming. Like Chłapowski, they stayed with Rennie at Phantassie and came back determined to revolutionise the farming on their own estates. They were faced with similar problems. To deal with complaints about the heaviness of Scots ploughs they offered a reward of two złoty to every peasant who became competent in the use of one. Other landowners were convinced that their farms could only be worked profitably by enforcing the *corvée*; the Zamoyskis abolished it and paid their labourers in cash. But, like Chłapowski, they discovered that importing foreign farmers and letting land on long leases was the most effective way of increasing the productivity of their estates.

Leases were modelled on those they had seen at Holkham. By the mid-1830s, many of the farmers originally settled at Dowspuda had become Count Andrzej's tenants. Andrew Broomfield and John Garvie were stewards at Greszczynska and Andrew Kedslie was at Michałów. These were to become the model farms on which the latest methods were demonstrated to neighbouring landowners and artificial fertilisers first used on Polish soil. Pedigree stock, seeds and machinery were sent directly from Britain by Andrzej's brothers, Władysław and Konstanty. After the failure of the 1830 Rising they both settled in Britain. When gathered to say farewell to Konstanty, after one of his rare visits to his Polish estates, the leader of the delegation of peasants is reported to have said:

> You had better get back to those Scots, master, from whom you said you had gained that knowledge by which we have profited so.[14]

By 1843 Count Andrzej, who remained in Poland, was able to hold the first Polish equivalent of a Holkham sheep-shearing at Klemenstow. Other landowners recognised that western techniques could be adapted to Polish conditions and paid labourers could profitably replace serfs. In eight years he had raised the income on the model farms from 11,000 to 52,700 złoty and reinvested 88,000 złoty in the estate.[15]

Cheese making was one of the practices introduced by the Scots. An eighteenth-century French traveller had complained that cheese was unobtainable. Amongst the tenant farmers, who were considered by Stanisław Zamoyski to practise 'exemplary farming and cattle raising', John Dickson was reported to be famous:

> ... an excellent breeder of pure bred cattle who produced yearly more than 500 quintals [53,638 British pounds] of excellent cheese

of the Cheshire type which was very much sought after by the urban population of Poland.[16]

Another of the Zamoyski tenants was Andrew Kedslie's cousin Alexander. He had come out in 1829 to manage the steam mill at Solec in Warsaw but by the 1830s was renting farms at Rozanice and Milanowich. He made over 240 entries connected with agriculture, gardening and veterinary science in his three surviving notebooks. They cover every aspect of farming practice – machinery, stock raising, seeds, dairying, fertilisers and management. Most are extracts from the innumerable technical journals to which he subscribed. There are eighteen pages on the analysis of soils; reports on experiments on the effect of four different types of manure on the yield of turnips at Gordon Castle in Morayshire and of deep ploughing potatoes at Pinkie Hill in Midlothian; a meticulous description of an improved American hay rake and a new method of dibbling turnips – 'one sturdy Scot with an improved hand dibble will go over an imperial acre in a day'. Typical is a long description by a Mr Chalmers of an experiment on feeding sheep. It concludes:

> Thus, with artificial food [oil cake] an acre of 30 tons will feed no less than 60 sheep, the artificial food will cost from 6d to 1/– each per week – suppose 9d. This will leave 7/6 for the half ton of turnips and a vast quantity of the very best manure.[17]

In 1846, when disease was devastating the potato crops in Ireland and Scotland, he sent resistant seed, raised on his own farm, back to the Horticultural Society in Britain.[18]

Farmers like Kedslie were tackling the basic problems of Polish farming. Land which had been impoverished by centuries of corn growing and superficial cultivation, starved of fertilisers and understocked, was being made productive. Their influence must have been considerable. By mid-century the most successful of them were buying estates. David Wilson owned several thousand acres near Lublin. During eleven years of heavy expenditure – draining 690 acres of heath and moss – he was able to keep going on the profits of his orchards and the distillery which was so often the mainstay of Polish estate economy. Potatoes, introduced by the Scots as a field crop, were being widely used for the distillation of vodka. He used British machinery and carried a stock of 30 oxen, 28 horses, 10 thoroughbreds for riding, 96 pure-bred cows and 3–800 Merino sheep.[19] Most estates were smaller; Strzyzew is probably typical. It consisted of two large farms near Warsaw rented by a Hay in the 1850s, then by a Govenlock, bought by Peter Garvie, the Żyrardów linen manufacturer, in the 1860s, managed by a Dickson and sold by the Garvies in 1907, after they had returned to Scotland. They practised model farming and built model cottages for their workers.

What was the legacy of these men? We know that, as tenants and managers, they enabled some of the great landowners to revolutionise the productivity and profitability of their estates. There were no Polish agricultural textbooks in the early nineteenth century but British farming methods were being described by the German agronomist A Thaer. His works were translated in Polish, and when Alojzy Biernecki translated both Louden's massive *Encyclopaedia of Agriculture* and many of Sir John Sinclair's writings on farming, landowners who never left home were able to study the theories underlying Scottish farming practices. In the 1830s Chłapowski publicised the results of his own adaptation of Scottish methods to Polish conditions; his textbook, which described the organisation of several Scottish estates, became a bestseller. Zamoyski's journal, the *Annals of National Agriculture*, first published in 1842, spread the message further. The impact of the Agricultural Society, which he founded in 1858, was enormous. Within a few years it had over 70 branches and 4,000 members. Niziol believes that it was 'by far the most valuable single initiative in Polish farming during the whole of the nineteenth century'. Its impact is reflected in grain exports. These increased tenfold between 1854 and 1862 and productivity of labour increased by 6.9% per annum between 1858 and 1863.[20] Unfortunately for the development of Polish agriculture the Society became involved in political activity. When the 1863 Rising failed, Zamoyski was exiled and the Society abolished. Productivity dropped and it was 1913 before it recovered to the 1863 level.[21] In the turbulent history of the twentieth century the impetus was lost. Polish farming in 1991 seemed little more advanced than Scottish farming between the two World Wars. Progress since then has been dramatic.

NOTES

1. J. Bartyś, 'English and Scottish Farmers in Poland', in *Agricultural History Review*, Vol. XV, 1997, 92.
2. J. C. Louden, *Encyclopaedia of Agriculture*, 100.
3. *Ibid*, 100.
4. K. Kretowska, 'Scotland in the Life of the Polish Country Estate', in C. T. Smout (ed.), *Scotland and Europe*, 173.
5. J. C. Louden, *op cit.*, 125.
6. Hay Letters 1819 (unpublished).
7. *Ibid*, 1824.
8. National Archives Suwałki, 1816–21.
9. J. Bartyś, quoted from *English Settlers in the Kingdom of Poland* (unpublished translation).
10. *Ibid*.
11. *Ibid*.
12. J. C. Louden, *op cit.*, 102.
13. K. Kretowska, *op cit.*, 185.
14. *Ibid*, 171.
15. S. Niziol, 'British Technology and Polish Development' (unpublished), 1994, 78.
16. J. Bartyś, *op cit*, 89.
17. A. Kedslie, Notebooks.
18. Consular Records F O 65/339 16.
19. J. Bartyś, *op cit.*, 90.
20. I. Kostrowika, 'Changes in Agricultural Productivity', in *Journal of European Economic History*, Vol. XIII, 49–50.
21. *Ibid*, 93.

CHAPTER SIX

The Gardeners

A century before they became 'Improvers', Scottish lairds were planting windbreaks to protect the gardens they were creating round their castles and mansions. Defence was no longer a primary consideration and gardens were becoming fashionable. At Stirling and Aberdour, in the sixteenth century, and Edzell in the early seventeenth, gardens were created with designs bought in France and seeds, bulbs and trees imported from England, France and the Netherlands. Gardening books proliferated. In Poland John Johnstone, the Scottish botanist who became court physician and a professor of medicine, was publishing treatises on plants and vegetables. Though born in Poland, he had studied at St Andrews and was familiar with developments in Scotland.

By the end of the century formal gardens were incorporated in the design of new houses. At Kinross the gardens were laid out and planted before Sir William Bruce started to build his Palladian mansion. Straight avenues of limes led up to the main entrance and, radiating from the house, created vistas from its state rooms. A parterre of box-edged beds was laid out in front of the windows and alleyways were decorated with classical sculptures. In the garden near Edinburgh which William Adam designed for the 1st Earl of Hopetoun, paved walks led to a round pond and grass rides to a temple or gazebo on rising ground at the edge of the park; in Lord Dundas's garden at Arniston in Midlothian the main vista led to a fountain, turned on in the evening to entertain guests at the dinner table. But by the mid-eighteenth century formal gardens were out of fashion. In one of his letters from Edinburgh Edward Topham registered their fall from favour:

Amongst the many improvements which have been encouraged in Great Britain within a few years, there is one which seems to have made as great a progress in this country as in England; I mean the improvement in taste in Gardening, Parks, Plantations and Pleasure Grounds, which is now directly opposite to what it was in the times of our fathers and grandfathers. I cannot look back but with astonishment, to find that it ever entered into the mind of man to imagine, that trees clipped into the resemblance of pillars and animals were beautiful or ornamental; and that the stiff formality of a gravel-walk terras, parterres divided into twenty regular figures, with a Cupid or a Mercury at each corner and a mixture of fountains, grottos, summer-houses and stone steps in the space perhaps of two acres could be pleasing or agreeable.[1]

By 1775 formal gardens were being replaced by landscaped 'English' parks. Parterres were ploughed up at Hopetoun and Arniston and 'natural' streams meandered through romantic gardens. Twenty years earlier the young Stanisław Poniatowski, before he became king, visited England. At Stowe in Buckinghamshire where, in 1730, William Kent had transformed the garden, Poniatowski upset the proud owner, Lord Temple, by regretting the disappearance of straight lines and canals. But he was sufficiently impressed to take back to Poland, and possibly to his mistress Catherine the Great of Russia, a copy of Benton Sealey's illustrated description of Stowe. He infected Catherine

21. The gardens at Branicki, 1995. Formal gardens like these went out of fashion when the Romantic movement swept across Europe in the late eighteenth century.

22. Princess Izabela Czartoryska. After her tour of Scottish gardens in 1793 the princess engaged James Savage to romanticise her gardens at Puławy.

with his enthusiasm and 'natural' gardens became the rage in Russia. Within a few years she had engaged British gardeners to transform the parks around her many palaces. Stowe's Palladian bridge was copied at Tsarsko Selo and Charles Cameron was commissioned to design the gardens as well as the house at Pavlovsk. The Russian nobility became 'gardening mad' and were reported to be offering salaries of £100 a year to 'English' gardeners.[2] This, at a time when graduate school teachers were often earning less than £30, was a salary which must have tempted many a needy Scot.

The fashion spread to Poland and was fuelled by the Romantic movement. The Scottish literary input was enormous. James Macpherson's *Ossian* was translated into French in 1774 and into Polish by 1782 and, to quote Katia Kretowska, 'The pan-European Ossianic epidemic swept the country'. Translations of James Thomson, Henry Mackenzie and Walter Scott followed. While Prince Adam Czartoryski toured factories and farms during their visit to Scotland in 1793, his mother, Princess Izabela, was collecting trophies for the Gothick folly she was to build in the park at her palace at Puławy. To relics collected from Fotheringhay, the site of Mary Queen of Scots' execution, she added stones from Holyrood, pictures of Fingal's Grave and Ossian's Tomb, and, still displayed nearly a century later, 'beneath glass, a blade of grass from Ossian's Tomb'. Other landowners engaged architects to design Scottish castles. In 1875 the journal *Klosy* described one built by the Italian F. M. Lanci for the Skrzynski family at Zagorzamy:

> Above the shade of an English park, there arises a rough-hewn building of six towers built in a square in the style of an old Scots castle, appearing as though reproduced directly from a novel by Walter Scott. In the light of the moon the castle creates a weirdly fantastic impression which is translated in the transparency of the lake.[3]

The writer Michael Grabowski lived in a folly which might have been modelled on Abbotsford. The Waverley Novels maintained a fashion for all things Scottish which lasted well into the mid-nineteenth century, when a periodical called the *Scottish Miscellany* was still finding readers for articles on Pictish sculptured stones and Scottish methods of tanning leather.

The influence of late eighteenth-century Scottish gardens on garden design in Poland must have been significant. The list of those seen by Princess Izabela in 1793 is formidable. She stayed at Tyninghame, recently romanticised, before going on to Edinburgh. After admiring the Botanic Gardens there, she visited Dalkeith Palace, Newbattle Abbey, Melville Castle and Hopetoun House. Travelling north, she saw Linlithgow, Scone, Dunkeld, Blair Atholl, Taymouth and Inveraray and finished her tour at Hamilton Palace. Her diary is full of descriptions of lakes, waterfalls, grottoes and Gothick follies. Ten years later her illustrated *Varied Thoughts on Ways of Designing Gardens* was the first Polish book on gardens to be published, and two editions were sold within a few years. There is no mention of gardeners but by that time her own garden at Puławy in south-east Poland had been transformed by the Scot, James Savage. When he died in 1820, she ordered an inscription for his gravestone which read:

> Here lies together with his son
> James Savage head gardener
> of the gardens at Puławy; his
> taste and superior talents
> could only be compared to his
> probity and untainted loyalty

The Irishman Denis McClair, who also worked at Pułway, went on to landscape the gardens of other Polish aristocrats in the Ukraine.[4]

Princess Izabela had admired the 'pittoresque' mountains and lochs of Scotland. The gardens she had inherited were still formal, French rather than English, and more appropriate for a 'Fête Champêtre' than a picnic in the country. The problem in Poland is that much of it is flat, part of the great European plain that stretches from East Anglia to the Urals. Earth has to be moved if a garden like Arkadia, which has been described as dripping with melancholy, is to be created. There its owner, Princess Helena Radziwillowa, could meditate alone in a temple dedicated to Diana under the lines:

> Oh! let me seek out some desolate shade
> And there weep my sad bosom empty.[5]

But with serf labour the problem could be solved: 300 men had been employed to landscape the gardens at Peterhof in Russia. A contemporary described how it was done at the Tauride Palace by William Gould, who had shown 'great judgement in forming the ponds, out of which he got sufficient materials to make the agreeable variety of swells and declivities'.[6] At Puławy a low range of hills made

23. Puławy: the Temple of the Sibyl. Lakes and miniature mountains were created and follies built. By the 1820s there were over 300 'English' gardens in Poland.

the site more promising and the course of the Vistula was altered 'to make it more irregular and craggy banked'. By 1824 there were over 300 English gardens in Poland.[6] The fashion spread from the parks of the aristocracy to the gardens of the gentry.

What part did Scottish gardeners play in creating these gardens? At home they had often had a high status. In the late seventeenth century William Frogg, the Earl of Cromartie's head gardener, wrote freely to his employer suggesting plants and bulbs which could be sent up from London for the gardens at Royston, near Edinburgh, and Tarbet, in Easter Ross. A few years later, letters from John Cockburn of Ormiston, one of the pioneers of agricultural improvement, suggest that his gardener was managing the estate while Cockburn pursued his political career in London. In Poland a landowner would have been more likely to leave the administration of his estate to an impoverished relative. But few Polish estate archives have survived destruction either by accident or design, and gardeners were servants whose names were in any case rarely recorded. In his recent research into the work of British gardeners in Russia, Anthony Cross found five Scottish names amongst the few recorded; in Poland I have found three. But Cross is convinced that there were many more. Describing the role of Catherine the Great, he wrote:

> Creating the fashion for English gardens among the Russian aristocracy she was also to create one for English, or rather British gardeners, since the majority were Scots. These gardeners are, however, unsung figures, rarely if ever mentioned or named, either in Russian or English accounts.[7]

Cross was writing about Russia but the same is almost certainly true of Scottish gardeners in Poland. By the early nineteenth century their reputation was as high as that of Scotland's farmers. There must have been many 'who arrived with an invitation, a letter of introduction or a ready business contract in their pockets'.[8] In his *Reminiscences of a Journey through England and Scotland*, which, like Czartoryska's book, was a bestseller, Szyrma described a visit to the Horticultural Society in Edinburgh in 1822:

As a rule Scottish gardening is at as high a level [as in England]

and is considered one of the first. This is the merit of the Horticultural Society which lavishly rewards good gardeners for first rate products. I was present at one of its yearly meetings combined with a dinner ... The Scottish gardeners are also considered the best and they are sent to England and even to the continent. The harshness of their own climate teaches them how to deal with plants with the greatest care. They know how to make the most of the soil and the climate.[9]

There is relatively little about gardening in the family papers although, from their letters, it is clear that many of them loved gardens. Kedslie made 24 entries in his notebooks. Typical are the description of a method of sprouting seeds before sowing, which nearly doubled the crop of onions on a two-and-a-half acre plot in 1840, and a note on the preservation of dahlia corms. The cost of moving different types of soil is calculated, a method of designing flowerbeds described and recipes for killing caterpillars, mice and moles noted. Lists of flowers and vegetables sown suggest that most of his seeds came directly from merchants in Britain:

> Hundredfold Potatoes from Gibbs & Co
> Hangdown Longpod Windsor Beans
> Myatts new Strawberry British Queen
> Milfords Marrow Pea – prolific

But seeds and plants from Scottish sources were advertised in Polish journals and it might have been possible to buy them in Warsaw. Tree seedlings had been imported from Keith Richmond's nursery near Edinburgh from the mid-eighteenth century, and Poles exiled after the 1830 Rising were exporting plants from Scotland to those of their family still in Poland in the mid-nineteenth century.

John Heiton, the designer of the gardens at Dowspuda, was remotely connected with my mother's family by the marriage of his daughter Alice to a Broomfield, one of the first of the farmers to settle on the estate. She appears in the consular records, probably applying for a passport, in March 1864. Her sister Margaret had married the architect Charles Marconi and is buried in the Marconi grave in Warsaw. Her declaration reads:

24. Dowspuda, 1995. At Dowspuda, the lake has almost silted up, and, of James Savage's garden, only the trees remain.

Certifying that Alice Heiton, widow Broomfield my sister, came to Poland along with my Father, Mother, and family in the year of our Lord 1819. Was born in Selkirk, Selkirkshire, Scotland in 1803 and has remained in Poland since 1819 until the present date during the above period in the year 1837 she was married to Mr George Broomfield who died in the year 1839 since which time she has remained a widow.[10]

Alice was a substantial donor to the funds of the Evangelical Reformed Church in the 1840s and appears to have been left relatively well-off, able to take part in the social life of the Scottish community.

Of her father the gardener I have found no personal records. At Dowspuda, the trees he planted and the lake he designed are still there but in a wilderness of wild flowers and uncut grass. He probably found the sandy soil and continental climate of Poland a considerable challenge. Jan Lindsay is credited with the design of the garden at Korsun, an early neo-Gothic mansion built in 1787 on one of the Poniatowski estates. He was born in Poland and was probably a second-generation emigrant from Scotland. Of James Savage I know even less. He died the year before the Heitons came out to Poland and was probably recruited by Princess Izabela in 1793. The inscription on his grave suggests that they became friends. Her palace at Puławy became a centre of cultural life and the home of the first Polish Museum of Remembrance. Savage's great romantic gardens are still there, overgrown and unkempt by British standards but an oasis of peace in what is now an industrial city. He and others like him were literate, experienced and enterprising and were able to make a substantial contribution to the development of gardening in Poland.

NOTES

1. E. Topham, *Letters from Edinburgh*, 226.
2. A. Cross, 'British Gardeners in Russia', in *Garden History*, Vol. 19, 1, 13.
3. K. Kretowska, 'Scotland in the Life of the Polish Country Estate', in T. C. Smout (ed.), *Scotland and Europe*, 181.
4. A Cross, *op cit.*, 15.
5. B Knox, 'The Landscape Garden in Poland and Bohemia', in *The Picturesque Garden and its Influence Outside the British Isles*, 109.
6. K. Kretowska, *op cit.*, 167.

7. A. Cross, *op cit.*, 15.
8. K. Kretowska, *op cit.*, 167.
9. L. Szyrma, *Reminiscences of a Journey through England and Scotland.*
10. Consular Papers 392/4.

CHAPTER SEVEN

The Miller

Amongst the hundreds of Scots who emigrated to Poland in the first quarter of the nineteenth century I have found only one miller, Alexander Kedslie. But more of his papers have survived than those of any of my other ancestors. His three notebooks cover the period from 1825 to 1872 and letters written to his grandson between 1864 and 1872 were treasured and brought back to Scotland in 1906. He appears in consular records and in family memoirs: my grand-uncle's published and my mother's in manuscript. Although his achievements were relatively unimportant, the breadth of his interests and his connections by marriage with so many of the Scottish families make his papers invaluable to an historian. They present a picture of a man of exceptional ability and integrity whose experiences must have mirrored those of many Scots whose lives were less well documented.

Kedslie was born in 1786 when milling techniques were beginning to change in Scotland. For centuries corn mills had been the property of landowners and a major source of income. Usually small, water-powered and primitive, using wooden gearing and wheels, they were leased to millers. Farming tenants were 'thirled' to the mill: in addition to having to take all grain grown on their land to the estate mill, they had to provide labour to build dams and sluices and to maintain the lades that brought water to the millwheel. Both the laird and the miller were entitled to a proportion of the meal ground. Millers were suspected of retaining more than their share and were notoriously unpopular. The agricultural revolution and the demand for flour by a growing urban population made the system obsolete. Ambitious millers moved into towns where large new mills could house the elevators and elaborate iron gearing necessary for improved productivity. Efficient kilns and granaries, where stored grain could stabilise flour and bread prices, were built and, by the 1780s, steam power was being introduced. At Dundee and Dunfermline this proved an expensive failure but, at Boulton and Watt's Albion Works in London, John

Rennie showed that it could be successfully adapted to milling. The installation of two 150-horsepower engines driving 20 pairs of stones increased productivity by 300%. 'Noble lords came and saw and in due course came back as customers with orders for mills.'[1]

Kedslie was one of this new generation of millers. His family had been small landowners in Lauderdale in the Borders since the twelfth century. His father Andrew, who was a younger son, moved to Leith where he became a corn merchant and miller and a burgess of Edinburgh. Alexander's burgess ticket was issued in 1807 'by right of his father'. By family tradition, Alexander started to study medicine at

25. Alexander Kedslie, 1786–1872. Kedslie went out to Poland in 1829 to manage the mills on the Potocki estate. He stayed to farm on the Zamoyski estate. His notebooks and letters have been an invaluable source of information about the life of the first-generation settlers in Poland.

Edinburgh University and made contact there with Count Aleksander Potocki during his first visit to Scotland in 1803. The entries in his notebooks – over 150 relating to medicine – suggest that this remained a lifelong interest. As a miller in Warsaw he would have been able to consult doctors; when farming many miles from the capital, emergency treatment of both accidents and serious illness in the household would have been normal. When his parents died in a typhoid epidemic, he took over the family business, and it was his younger brother who became the doctor in the family.

Very little had been written about milling until the late eighteenth century, so Kedslie's notebook entries were probably particularly important for his work. Robertson Buchanan's *Treatise on Milling* was published at the end of the century and Oliver Evans' *Young Miller and Millwright's Guide* went into thirteen editions in America in the 1830s. This was one of many technical books and journals whose publisher and price were carefully noted by Kedslie. The earliest entries in the surviving notebook from 1825 are about milling: 'To calculate the power of overshot water-wheels' for example, and 'Brass, the strength necessary for pulley blocks, wheels, spindles etc.'. On the preservation of grain he wrote:

> To preserve Rye and secure it from insects and rats nothing more
> is necessary than to winnow it after it is thrashed and to store it
> in the granneries mixed with the chaff. In this state it has been
> kept for three years without experiencing the slightest alteration
> and even without the necessity of being turned to preserve it
> from humidity and fermentation.[2]

The dimensions of the mill at Duddingston are given with meticulous care. This was a water mill in a village outside Edinburgh. Nearer to town, on the Water of Leith, the Kedslies rented the Bonnington Mills. These had been equipped with the most up-to-date iron machinery in the 1780s and in 1814 a steam engine was installed. The inhabitants of Stockbridge protested. In a petition dated November 1814, they claimed that the amenities and advantages of their village as a growing suburb of Edinburgh were threatened 'by the nuisance due to the copious emission of very foul smoke from the chimney of the steam mill erected beside the water mill'. Kedslie replied courteously

26. The Steam Mill, Solec, *c.* 1915. The 60-horsepower steam engine installed at the mill was probably assembled by William Preacher at the Solec engineering works. It was for many years the most powerful in Poland.

that the nuisance was due to inexperience and would not continue.[3] The painter Henry Raeburn, previously a family friend, complained that his wife's washing green was being covered with soot. He took the case to law and engaged Henry Cockburn, the author of *Memorials of his Time*, to represent the petitioners. Kedslie appealed to the Court of Session not to discourage such a step forward as the adoption of steam power. His counsel, Francis Jeffrey, the editor of the *Edinburgh Review*, brought the professional washerwomen of Stockbridge into court to swear that their washing was not being affected; how, then, could Mrs Raeburn's? Jeffrey convinced the jury but it may have been an expensive victory for Kedslie.

When he installed the steam engine, he was still a very wealthy man. In 1806 Napoleon's Continental System had closed the ports of France and her allies to British goods; Britain retaliated with the Orders in Council to prevent France from trading with neutral countries. At a time when Britain was becoming increasingly dependent on imported food and foreign markets, corn prices soared and many industries

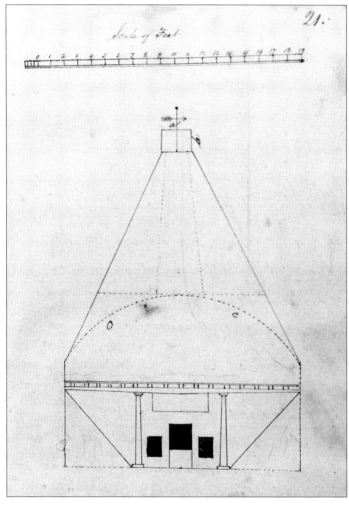

27. Diagram of a Kiln. One of many technical drawings from Kedslie's
notebooks.

suffered. Breaking through the double blockade, Kedslie landed two
cargoes of Scottish goods at Danzig; the Baltic corn he brought back
was sold at Leith when corn prices were at their highest. Two years
later, when the blockades were lifted and prices plummeted after
Waterloo, he is believed to have lost £30,000 on cargoes of wheat
bought in America. He struggled on till 1829 but his finances never
recovered. When Count Potocki invited him to take over the

management of the steam-mill at Solec in Warsaw, he was more than ready to leave Scotland.

On their visits to Britain the Polish aristocrats had probably visited the steam-powered Albion Works in London. Those who reached Scotland and stayed with George Rennie at Phantassie would certainly have inspected the nearby mill where Andrew Meikle was the miller and John Rennie, George's brother, had served an apprenticeship. These were two of the most distinguished engineers of their generation. Meikle, who had invented the machine which revolutionised threshing, toured Britain advising on new milling techniques. Rennie, after studying mathematics at Edinburgh University, carried out major engineering works throughout Britain, amongst others enlarging Leith docks and building four of the bridges over the Thames. This was the environment in which Kedslie developed confidence in his own skills. Within two days of reaching Warsaw he was clearly taking charge of the steam mill at Solec. In the first notebook the entry 'Arrived Warsaw July 10th 1829' is followed by 'Particulars regarding Mills etc at Warsaw furnished by Mr Kremsky 12th July 1829'.

Traditionally, Poland had exported corn, not flour, and Britain had become her main market. The Corn Laws, introduced in 1815 to protect British farmers from competition, had seriously damaged this trade. Foreign corn could not be imported till the home price reached 80/− a quarter; this happened so rarely in peacetime that it virtually excluded Polish corn from the British market. Since there was no restriction on the import of flour, the government of the Congress Kingdom set up a Company to Export Flour in 1825. This served the overland Russian market and flour was also exported to London and Glasgow through Danzig. It was to meet this growing demand that Count Potocki decided to modernise his mills.'Improvers' like Pac and the Zamoyskis had been installing new machinery in their mills; Potocki was the first to invest in steam power.

The 60-horsepower engine supplied by the state engineering works at Solec was one of the first, and certainly the largest, to be assembled by the team of technicians recruited in Britain in 1825. William Preacher may have supervised the work. The dimensions of the engine and those of the machinery it drove were meticulously recorded by Kedslie in 1829:

DIMENSIONS OF SEVERAL PARTS OF THE MACHINES IN
THE STEAM MILL, WARSAW

The Mill is driven by a Steam Engine of 60 horses power. It makes sixteen strokes a minute and drives 8 pairs of stones of 4 feet 4 inches in diameter. Length of stroke of the Engine 7 feet.

Two further pages detailing measurements of the machinery at Solec are followed by the dimensions of other mills on the Potocki estates – the watermills at Augustowa and Kociowka, of a horse-driven mill at Stul and a smaller 30-horsepower steam-mill at Modlin.

There are pages on 'The Power of Steam Engines and the Method of Computing it'. Other entries deal with productivity and costs. By the end of July he had recorded the quantity and quality of flour produced and the running costs of the mill:

PRODUCE OF 1083 KORZEC OF CLEAN RYE 20TH JULY 1829
[1 korzec = 3.49 bushels]

Rye	213.150	
Produce		
Fine		84.800
Second		15.358
Third		7.405
Fourth		19.006
Bran		78.960
Waste		7.621
		213.150

90½ Klafters [1 Kl = 2122 lbs] of wood burned during 92 hours which was occupied in grinding the above

	FLORINS	GROSCHEN
Wood cost		
	1513	11
Expenses of establishment	1153	21
	2651	21

The same quantity by A K produced at the same price 4000 fl more.

There are several notes of a similar nature.'When Mr Tribuit came
to the Mill he said he could produce from 100 lbs of wheat 70lbs of
fine [flour] ... on trial he produced 33 lbs.' We are not told what
happened to Mr Tribuit nor do we know how Kedslie communicated

28. Dimensions of the Mill at Augustowa. The machinery and the
performance of the mills for which he became responsible were
minutely described within a few months of Kedslie's arrival in Poland.

with him and the other 36 men employed at the mill. He noted that they were paid 60 florins a month and that the mill ran for 20 hours a day but there is nothing about their working hours or living conditions.

The problems facing Kedslie and other foreigners who came to Poland as managers must have been enormous. Polish is amongst the most difficult of European languages for an English speaker to learn and senior managers must have had to master Russian and German as well. A Russian-English dictionary and phrase book, published in Moffat in 1772, came back to Scotland in 1906 but there is nothing similar in Polish. There may have been a Polish community in Leith amongst whom Kedslie found a teacher – it is difficult to imagine him planning to emigrate to Poland without making a serious attempt to learn the language – but his letters suggest that till the end of his life he spoke and thought in English. There is not a word of Polish in the notebooks, but there are pages of conversion tables for every type of English-Polish measurement. These are amongst the earliest entries in the notebooks.

For farmers the language problem would have been less serious. Most of them settled in communities of Scots and worked with their families and friends, employing only a few Poles. Many of the Polish landowners spoke English as well as French – Englishness was fashionable and Walter Scott widely read amongst the upper classes. There would have been English speakers on all the major estates and the mastery of Polish was less urgent for the farmers than it was for men like Kedslie and other engineers.

The picture which emerges from Kedslie's notes is that of a conscientious and efficient manager. Coal in Warsaw cost three times its pit-head price and was of poor quality. Although he noted that 'It requires 3 lbs of dry pine wood to have the same effect as 1 lb of coal', peat and other woods were even less efficient and there was no alternative to dry pine. The engine used '1 Klafter or 2122 lbs English or 2387 Polish lbs an hour'. Running costs were high. Contrasting the expenses of the steam-mill with a watermill in the country, Kedslie reckoned that the steam-mill at Solec cost 703 florins, 28 groschen more per day to run and concluded:

The Mill working 280 days per annum and producing 140 barrels of flour per day shows that flour costs £1.5 per barrel more by steam than by water. The expense of each horse power is £6.3 per day.

In 1834 he was carrying out trials with different mixtures of undried, kiln-dried and fanned wheat to find the most profitable mixture. A typical entry is:

NO. 2   5TH MARCH

200 Kor wheat net weight	46.661
Waste in cleaning	.482
	46.179
Waste in grinding and cleaning	.488
	45.691

PRODUCE

Fine flour	29.561
Second	1.232
Thirds	7.097
Fourths	2.980
Bran	4.821
	45.691

REMARKS

Ground in 10¾ hours   10½ Klafters wood used
½ quart machinery oil   2½ lbs Tallow
1½ lbs Soft soap and tallow 2½ lbs Alum
Wheat mixed with Kiln dried

RETURNED 15TH MARCH

59^{23}⁄$_{32}$ lbs per English bushel

Kedslie was still managing the Mill in 1835, but by this time Potocki was a refugee and the Flour Company was bankrupt. Its early success is recorded in the figures Kedslie noted for flour imported by Britain. Between 1826 and 1829 London's imports increased from 1,437 barrels to 66,689 and Liverpool's from 30,200 to 160,000. But the company lost several cargoes as a result of accidents when shipping flour abroad and the Russian market was closed after the 1830 Rising. In 1836 the mill was taken over by Piotr Steinkeller, a Polish industrialist with a genius for backing unsuccessful ventures.[4] Whether Kedslie left the mill by choice or was dismissed is not recorded. He became a farmer but his interest in every aspect of milling remained. There are over 80 entries in this connection in the notebooks and there are detailed descriptions of his cousin's papermill at Celajów, and of thrashing-, bone- and sugarbeet-mills in other parts of Poland.

His interest in the development of steam power was equally long-lived. By family tradition, he helped to train the first generation of Polish train drivers on the line linking Częstochowa to Warsaw and Vienna. There are nine entries in the notebooks recording the amount of fuel used. On October 7th and 8th it was 'from Warsaw to Częstochowa and back with No 7 Locomotive; windy weather. Burned 29 quarters of wood – to 1566 feet Polish – 4 gallons of oil'. On October 14th and 15th 'with the Grand Duke', and presumably less wind, they burned only 27 quarters. He probably acted as a consultant. The British technical journals to which he subscribed kept him in touch with western developments and his copies circulated amongst the foreign community. His influence as a highly skilled engineer and miller must have survived long after he left the steam-mill, doubtless a very disappointed man.

It was several years after I had indexed his notebooks that I found Kedslie's letters to my grandfather, Thomas Garvie, who was sent to school in Edinburgh – first to Mr Hunter's preparatory school in York Place and then to the Edinburgh Institution in Queen Street – when he was 12 years old. The notebooks are completely impersonal; from the letters he emerges as a loving and deeply religious man. By 1864 he was 75 and was living in retirement with his daughter Jane and her husband Peter Garvie. When Jane and her baby died the following year, Kedslie became increasingly important in the lives of the eight surviving children. Thomas was the eldest. He boarded with a Mr and Mrs Smart and, after his mother's death, moved to his father's uncle and aunt, the Sinclairs. He must have been a very lonely little boy and Kedslie always gave him family news. This extract is about his young brother Alfred who was to become a distinguished theologian; when Thomas left home he was a baby:[5]

Alfred has become a complete speaking machine and with a boundless imagination concocts the most wonderful stories to the amusement of all the house; did I attend to all his demands to draw him men horses and doggies I would have my time fully occupied. One thing he has determined that he is going, when he is bigger, to stay with Tommy.

Alfred grew up to adore his grandfather. In his autobiography he recounts his dismay when he took a broken glass to his room and discovered that there was something his grandfather could not mend.

There was also much good advice. In one of Kedslie's first letters to Thomas he wrote:

I see from the enumeration of your lessons that you will not have much time to spare; a little custom will however I trust enable you to get through them so that you will have time to take such exercise for the benefit of your health as is needful. To this you must sacrifice your love of reading. What you do read let it be as much as possible of a useful nature. I trust that you will not neglect to read a portion of the *New Testament* and whatever other time you have mostly read History, Travel and Voyages, Biography etc which are both profitable and amusing.

A few months later he was writing:

I hope you are not forgetting your German ... I take it for probable it will either be in the Mercantile or Mechanical branches you will enter life in both the same branches of education are useful, only in the last named a higher attainment in Mathematics and Mechanical drawing would be necessary; modern languages are of the greatest importance in both.

When he moved to the Institution, Kedslie was concerned because Thomas had not mentioned drawing. He hoped he would find time to attend lectures in Chemistry but continued:

Do not think dear Boy that I want you to fill up all your time in learning take time for healthful exercise and learn fewer branches at a time ... forgive me if I seem to give you so many advices but I hope you believe that I am actuated by love for your future welfare both in spiritual and temporal things.

Thomas's letters to his grandfather have not survived. It would be interesting to know how he responded to a query about church politics – 'Is it likely that a union will take place between the Free and United Churches?' – or about the art scene in Edinburgh:

> You mention that Mr Smart had pictures for sale in the Exhibition did he get a good price for them? There were two brothers of the name of Lauder who were intimate in my father's family who adopted painting as a profession and were said to possess talent – ask Mr Smart if they live and if they have succeeded in their persuits.

Both the brothers, James Eckford and Robert Scott Lauder, had in fact succeeded and Mr Smart would certainly have known them. More difficult to deal with was Kedslie's next request:

> And now I have to ask you to do a little business matter. You know your father is very fond of fish. I was telling him that I used to receive dried ones from Shetland in return for goods I sent there and that they used not to be dear. Could you find out from anybody in Leith or Edinburgh their present price per Cwt or Ton, the kind I mean are dried Cod or Ling or such other dried fish that would bear transportation to this country. If you have no other means of information perhaps Mrs Sinclair could assist you to procure it.

A few months later, after congratulating him on prize-wining exam results, he wrote:

> I think of writing to you in two or three days time a communication concerning the cattle disease containing a mode of cure which is said to have been successful in Russia and which you can send to the Scotsman or some of the other papers.

These must have been tough assignments even for a prize-winning and earnest twelve-year-old.

In the letter he wrote on the day his daughter died Kedslie's personality comes through most clearly. On the cover there is a note to Mr Sinclair: 'Please do not give Tommy this note until you have given him the sad news contained in his Father's. Ever yours A K'. He concludes:

> ... I would that I could have been with you when you read these lines that I might endeavour to sooth those feelings which must have pervaded your heart when your unexpected loss was made known to you and which no doubt still endure but alas! my dearest Boy I can find no comfort for myself. On my knees I have asked submission from my saviour and my God and to say Thy Will be Done but the rebel heart will not be quieted – God forgive me the sin. O my Boy in this hour of your trial seek to the Lord and he will sustain you for he hath said Although Father and Mother forsake you (or be taken from you) the Lord will take you up.

NOTES

1. E. Gauldie, *The Scottish Country Miller, 1700–90*, 145.
2. A. Kedslie, Notebooks (unpublished).
3. A. E. Garvie, *Memories and Meanings of my Life*, 17.
4. S. Niziol, *British Technology and Polish Development*, 115.
5. Garvie Letters, 1864–68 (unpublished).

CHAPTER EIGHT

The Political Background

Alexander Kedslie was one of the few emigrants who might have had
a vote in a parliamentary election before he left Scotland. As a burgess
and a merchant he could have been a member of the City Council,
the self-perpetuating oligarchy which elected the MP for Edinburgh.
In a population of around two million, the franchise in Scotland was
restricted to 4,439 people. Henry Dundas, the 'Satrap of Scotland',
had boasted that, given time, he would have all 46 MPs elected in
the 1796 election in the government's pocket. He failed by one
member: Sir David Carnegie, MP for Fife and a personal enemy,
continued his support of the Whig opposition. In 1785 William Pitt
had himself introduced a bill to abolish some of the grosser abuses in
the system and in 1789 the most intelligent of the Tories, men like
Edmund Burke, welcomed the Revolution in France. But by 1793
the 'Friends of the People', an association advocating constitutional
reform, had been banned by Pitt's government and its leaders sentenced
to transportation. All trade union activity was made illegal, Habeas
Corpus was suspended and repression became increasingly severe during
the years of the postwar depression. In England there were the Peterloo
Massacre and the Tolpuddle Martyrs and in Scotland the Radical War.
The country the Scots left behind them was governed by an undemo-
cratically elected and corrupt government.

There is no evidence to suggest that any of the emigrants was a
political refugee but, to those who were politically aware, the Congress
Kingdom must have been a startling contrast to Britain. Its constitution
had been drawn up by Prince Adam Jerzy Czartoryski, one of the
most powerful aristocrats in Poland. His family had had close connections with Scotland since the early eighteenth century when an ancestor
had married a Gordon of Huntly. His father, Prince Adam Kazimierz,
had toured Scotland from the Borders to the Orkneys and studied
British institutions under the guidance of Lord Mansfield, the distinguished Scottish judge who became Lord Chief Justice of England.

Inspired by what they had seen, he and his wife Princess Izabela became pioneers in their attempts to modernise the economies of their estates and emancipate their peasants. When Adam Jerzy was sent to Britain in 1789, his father wrote: 'The main purpose of the journey is to gather material necessary for the moment when you are chosen to serve your Motherland'. The moment came 25 years later when the czar Alexander I asked him to advise on the creation of a constitution for the Congress Kingdom.

Alexander had been a critic of his grandmother Catherine the Great's treatment of Poland, an admirer of Napoleon's reforms, and a would-be liberal who dreamt of bringing democratic government to all his dominions. Prince Adam and his brother had been living in Moscow since the final Partition in 1795. The Czartoryski estates had been forfeited as punishment for supporting Kosciuszko's unsuccessful Rising against the Partitioning powers; restoration was conditional on the brothers' residence in Russia as hostages. Prince Adam had returned from Britain as staunch an anglophile as his father; to live in Catherine's court must have been a devastating experience. To quote the Polish historian W. Liponski:

> Here we have a young worshipper and enthusiast for English democracy ... who went almost directly from the capital of European liberalism to czarist Russia, a country dominated by autocracy and extreme despotism. From the motherland of brilliant economic progress, independent courts and effective administration – to the centre of primitive feudalism, unlimited licence of the 'blagorodye' over their serfs, bribed magistrates and inefficient supervisors.[1]

Although the Czartoryskis were in Russia as hostages, Adam and the young czar became friends. Close study of the theory and an idealised picture of the practice of British politics lay behind the constitution which they drew up for the Congress Kingdom. On his return from the peace talks in Paris in 1814, Alexander is reported to have said to an assembly of Poles at Vilna, 'Gentlemen, yet a little patience and you will be more than satisfied with me'.[2] He retained the Code Napoléon as the basis of the legal system, promised liberty of press and person to the Poles and allowed them their own army as well as control of education and the economy. The State Council

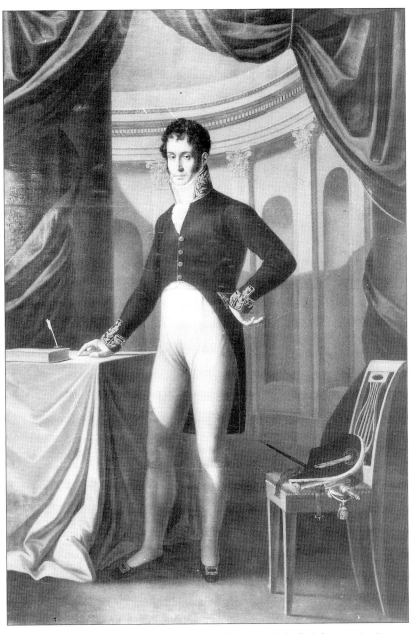

29. Prince Adam Czartoryski, 1770–1861. Czartoryski drafted the constitution
granted by Alexander I to the Congress Kingdom in 1815. Nicholas I's failure to
respect the constitution led to the unsuccessful 1831 Rising and to the exile or death
of those who had taken part in it.

was appointed by the czar and drafted all laws. Although the two-chamber parliament, the Sejm, was to meet for only two months every second year and then only to make 'petitions and interpolations' on these laws, it was an elected assembly with an unusually liberal franchise. The Kingdom must have seemed to the Scottish emigrants as promising politically as it was economically.

Long before his death Alexander I had become disillusioned with democracy. When the Sejm became critical of measures proposed by the State Council it was dissolved. Censorship was introduced in 1819 and the Polish governor, General Zajeczek, was increasingly overruled by the reactionary viceroy, the Archduke Constantine, Nicholas I, who succeeded to the throne in 1825, was as reactionary as his viceroy. The press was muzzled and his repressive policies and brutal treatment of the army drove the Poles into revolt. During the 1830 Rising the Polish army met the invading Russian troops with munitions supplied by the Solec factory. This was managed by William Preacher but most of the Scots played no direct part in the revolt.[3] Like Kedslie, they probably believed that domestic politics were not the concern of foreigners. The British government had protested at the time of the Partitions but gave no effective help to the Poles. The pattern was repeated in 1830 and 1863.

During the period after 1831 British residents must have become increasingly aware of the serious impact of political change on their own lives. The Congress Kingdom survived in name only. By the Organic Statue, Nicholas I suspended the constitution and set out to destroy the economy as well as every aspect of Polish culture. The Rising had been led by aristocrats, many of whom had been in the van of economic progress. Their estates were confiscated. Led by Adam Czartoryski, few of the 10,000 who escaped to western Europe and made Paris their headquarters came back. For the survivors of the 180,000 deported to Siberia there was no amnesty till 1855. The effect on the Congress Kingdom was devastating. It is summed up by Niziol:

> The political extinction of the country occurred precisely at the moment when new intellectual trends had awakened a desire for reform and reconstruction, when an economic revival was gaining momentum, when trade was increasing and education expanding.

L.PAC.

30.   General Ludwik Pac, 1780–1835. Pac was a leader of the Rising. His exile to France terminated the economic development of the Dowspuda estate in which the Scots had played so prominent a part.

Early settlers from Scotland had been financed by the aristocracy; after 1830 the Bank Polski became the only major source of finance. But the Bank had to find money for half the cost of the Russian army of occupation and, itself short of capital, it starved enterprises started in the 1820s. The enforced closure of universities and technical colleges made Poland more than ever dependent on foreign experts but recruiting became increasingly difficult. The conditions that had attracted the Scots to the Congress Kingdom no longer existed; they found themselves under a military dictatorship in a world of broken contracts and shrinking markets.

During the Crimean War the remaining Scots must have kept their heads very low. Consular records suggest moments of panic.[4] In March 1854, 43 Govenlocks, Hays, Dicksons and Burns living in the district of Stanislaus near Warsaw applied to have their passports renewed. Andrew Broomfield and Anna Garvie farmed land some distance from Warsaw. On June 25th 1854 five of their children, who had been born between 1835 and 1846, were brought to be christened in the Evangelical Reformed Church in Warsaw and were registered as British citizens at the Consulate. The official policy since 1820 had been to encourage the establishment of foreign firms and the employment of foreign experts. This was reversed in the 1850s and the Evans Brothers' engineering company, the most successful of foreign ventures, was transferred to Lilpop and Rau, Poles who had been trained in the Evans' factory. By the end of the century aliens who did not apply for Russian nationality were expelled. Directors of factories, the Austrian Karl Dittrich and Peter Garvie at Żyrardów, for example, were exempt but managers came under the expulsion order. Thomas Garvie, at that time a manager in the factory, led other senior personnel in refusing to apply. So many of these were foreigners – French, Austrian, German, Swiss as well as British – that the Russian government realised that they were irreplaceable in management and the order was never enforced. In other parts of Poland foreigners were expelled.

In 1838 Kedslie had complained to the British Consul General of the lawlessness of guards on the Galician border; in 1863 Thomas Govenlock was bringing more serious charges against Russian soldiers near Warsaw. The Govenlocks had been shepherds rather than farmers in Scotland but Thomas's father Walter became one of the successful tenant farmers on the Dowspuda estate. Most of his family moved south after the 1830 Rising and by the 1850s were buying their own farms. Thomas's letter from his estate at Sionna is worth quoting at length for the light it throws on conditions under Russian rule.

A military road or *szosse*, from Warsaw to the fortress of Brześć, ran through his estate. Writing to the Consul on June 18th, he complained:

> We have got quite accustomed to be badly used and harassed by the Russian soldiery continually moving one way or the other along the road, but now it is quite unsufferable and not only am I forced to submit to damages done to my crops by the Cossacks riding through them every two or three days to the right and left of the Szosse, pulling down fences and sometimes riding through (for nothing but an inclination to do damage) fruit, kitchen and flower gardens on horseback and not only that but for peace's sake a person is forced to supply them with whatever they demand, Hay, Straw and Corn for their horses and meat and drink for themselves, and glad to be quit of them without receiving from them by way of payment a few touches of their Bat. Of course these demands are made by stragglers and not in the presence of any Officer but most certainly with their knowledge. But all that I would have let pass unnoticed as in that respect I am no worse situate than my neighbours but the cowardly and Brutal manner the Cossacks acted yesterday towards my son (a Boy of eighteen years of age) is quite unsufferable and cannot be let pass without some kind of redress. Yesterday between the hours of one and two afternoon my son and eight men were returning to their work in the fields after dinner, my son some distance behind the men at the time a company of Cossacks of from forty to fifty were passing along the Szosse when ten Cossacks left the company and rode straight across the fields in the direction of my son, who stood still as soon as he saw they were after him, three of them immediately laid hold of him cursing and insulting him in the Russian language, my son told them that he was an Englishman – they said they knew what he was and swore that he was the Commander of a Band of Rebels or Bandosiks and they would have him so one ordered three to hold him while a forth lashed him most unmercifully with his whip or Bat the other six rode after the men going to work and after beating several of them ordered the whole to march with them to Warsaw.

I met them as they returned to the Szosse. I told them that I was an Englishman and that my son and those were my people but they only cursed me and said that if that was my son that I must also be a rebel and ordered me to march along with them to Warsaw. So after going some distance they proposed to me to pay them some money and they would let us go. So I was forced to accept their proposals and get free by paying them some four or five florins and so the matter ended. There was no officer with the ten that committed the outrage, but it is most probable that there was an Officer with the company on the Szosse who by this time had passed on, but of that I am not certain, it happened on Wednesday the 17th of June ... My estate is worth 45,000 roubles let the Russian Government pay me my Estate and I will leave the country and be no more trouble to them.

Thomas Govenlock

Sionna by Waleszyn [5]

This was during the 1863 Rising but A E Garvie's description of life in Poland in the latter part of the century, when Poland had become a province under direct rule, suggests that the corruption, if not the flagrant lawlessness, continued. He summarised the political situation as 'tyranny tempered by bribery' and said it left him with a lifetime distrust of government and officialdom. They stood in his mind for tyranny, bribery and violence.[6]

The bitterness of 1863 was the greater because the accession of Alexander II in 1855 had led to a real change in Russian policies in Poland. He believed that 'The happiness of Poland is to be found in complete fusion with the people of my Empire'.[7] The brutally repressive Archduke was replaced by the 'friendly Viceroy' Gorchakof and the Polish Council of State was restored. Trade barriers had been removed in 1851. The humiliation of defeat in the Crimean War had convinced the government that the economy must be modernised. The railway system was at last developed to link industrial regions with sources of raw material, and goods manufactured in Poland could reach vast and rapidly growing markets in Russia and the Far East. During this period of 'The Thaw' agricultural progress was also

PUNCH, OR THE LONDON CHARIVARI.—FEBRUARY 21, 1863.

A GROWL FOR POLAND.

Mr. BULL. "AH OLD DOG—YOU'D LIKE TO HAVE ANOTHER RUN AT THAT BEAR, WOULDN'T YOU: BUT IT WON'T DO THIS TIME."

31. *Punch*, February 1863. The British government was sympathetic towards the Polish Risings, both in 1831 and 1863, but made no attempt to assist the insurgents. Tenniel cartoon.

impressive. Zamoyski's Agricultural Society, founded in 1857, was still advocating Scottish practices and seemed set to transform Polish farming. Tragically, the Society became political. There was still no legal outlet for Polish aspirations and the Society seems to have played a role not unlike that of the Roman Catholic Church under the Communists in twentieth-century Poland. Its petition for the redress of political grievances was dismissed by Alexander and the Society was dissolved in 1861.

The Thaw had been short-lived. The imposition of conscription led to another armed rising in 1863 but this time there was no Polish army with trained officers to lead the revolt. In spite of this, a courageous underground movement resisted the Russian government for over a year. Retribution was inevitable. The Congress Kingdom disappeared and was replaced by the Vistula Territory, a province of the Empire. Russian became the language of primary as well as higher education, and when Catholics were barred from senior administrative posts, most Poles were excluded. Repression continued till the 1905 Revolution threatened the entire Russian Empire and the czar was forced to make some concessions to democratic and national demands.

The Scottish community was much more closely involved in 1863 than it had been in the 1830 Rising. A few played an active part and suffered for it. In 1866 the Foreign Ministry informed the British consul that Thomas Dickson, grandson of a Dowspuda settler, was 'expelled from Poland for having fought Russia during the uprising'.[8] In spite of the consul's protests, William Preacher's nephew was executed for driving a train which was leading a convoy bringing supplies to the insurgents.[9] Peter Garvie, who remembered as a child hiding in the forest during the 1830 Rising, protected both Poles and Scots in 1863. He shut his eyes to the revolutionary activities going on around him and gave practical help to the insurgents when he could. As a managing director of the Żyrardów linen works, he was able to find a job in the factory for a Scot in danger of capture and sheltered him in his own house. A squad of Russian soldiers was sent to search his house but the officer in command was a Persian aristocrat. He had been sent to school in England and, when stationed in Żyrardów during the Rising, had become a friend of the English-speaking Garvie family. He decided not to recognise the Scot, in bed and pretending to be asleep, and a few weeks later Garvie was able to smuggle him out of the country. Two of the Kedslie sisters who lived in Warsaw were involved in covering up the rooftop escapes of Polish insurgents, hiding them in garrets while neighbouring houses were searched.[10] Treasuring their British passports, most of the immigrants kept out of politics, but there is ample evidence to show where their sympathies lay.

There was no amnesty for the thousands of insurgents deported to Siberia. In despair, most of the Poles who escaped capture and trial turned their backs on politics and put their energy into economic development and local government. Experience of work in the *zemstvas*, elected councils set up by the czar to undermine the influence of landowners, increased the confidence of a growing middle class. The economy took off and by the 1890s Russia was on the gold standard and had become attractive to foreign investors. Poland, the Vistula Territory, became the most industrialised province in the Empire.

Serfdom in Poland was abolished in 1864 on terms rather less favourable than those granted to serfs in Russia. Peasants were desperately poor and provided almost unlimited cheap labour for industry, but illiteracy and ignorance remained high as long as primary education was in the Russian language. Trade unions were illegal and long hours and low pay normal. Since the 1887 factory laws, intended to protect labour, were soon modified in favour of employers and were largely unenforced, industrial towns became major recruiting areas for the new and rapidly growing international socialist labour movements. The textile industry, where thousands of workers were employed, was infiltrated by agents from the Social Democratic Workers' Party and, for the first time, Polish opposition to Russia was associated with an industrial proletariat drawn from the peasant classes. When strikes started in the 1880s and 1890s in Łódź and Żyrardów, those Scots who had become employers looked to the government for support against organised violence.

It was 1905 before paternalistic employers like Thomas Garvie recognised the link between strike action and Polish claims to independence and found their loyalties divided. He had followed his father Peter as a managing director of a firm employing over 9,000 people. On June 26th 1905 he wrote to his daughter Jean, then a student in London:

> ... As far as we can hear there is not the slightest wish amongst them [the workers] to cause any disturbance, so that there is ever hope that we shall not be affected by the movement in Łódź [the centre of the cotton textile industry] and elsewhere. In Łódź there appears to be a complete state of anarchy, it is no longer a movement against the manufacturers but against the government. As the mob are now firing at the public and soldiers from revolvers, it is no wonder that they shoot in return.[11]

Jean was allowed to return to Poland in the autumn when industrial unrest appeared to have subsided. She was a conservative and a perfervid Scot but in 1905 clearly identified with the Poles. On November 11th she wrote to her brother Peter, who had been sent to school in England when the situation in Żyrardów became dangerous, describing 'Freedom Day' when, for the first time since 1863, expressions of national identity were legalised:

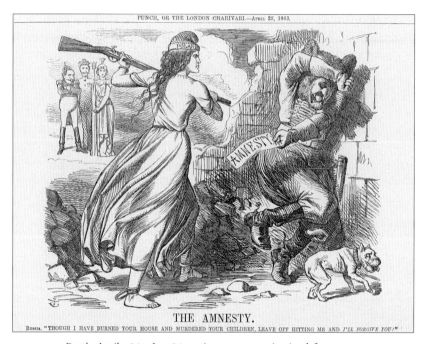

PUNCH, OR THE LONDON CHARIVARI.—April 25, 1863.

THE AMNESTY.

Russia. "THOUGH I HAVE BURNED YOUR HOUSE AND MURDERED YOUR CHILDREN, LEAVE OFF HITTING ME AND *I'LL FORGIVE YOU!*"

32. *Punch,* April 1863. In 1863 resistance was maintained for over a year.
An amnesty was never granted to the thousands of Poles who were exiled to Siberia.
Tenniel cartoon.

We had grand celebrations of freedom on Monday last. There
were 27 flags with Polish eagles. We just yelled 'Beze ces Polske'
[Poland still lives] in the streets. It was a grand show, about 20,000
people with nobody crushed or killed and no police. Cowdy and
Kennedy [Irish managers in the factory] ran about after the flags
of the [factory] departments. We sent Pater to the Lutheran
Church and represented him at the Catholic business. In the
evening we had two candles in every window and four in mine
to crown the edifice.

The concessions Alexander III had been forced to make after the
Revolution were being eroded by 1914. As a province of Russia,
Poland was swept into the war. She again became a battleground.
Russia withdrew from the war in 1917, and when Poland emerged
as an independent republic after Versailles her industrial areas and
infrastructure had been devastated. Many of the Scots had escaped;

some who remained were killed. Thomas Garvie returned from retirement in Scotland to salvage what he could of the firm's property and died in Murmansk in 1918. Almost all the emigrants had seen their own and their parents' achievements destroyed and were financially ruined.

NOTES

1. W. Liponski, 'The Influence of Britain on Prince Adam Jerzy Czartoryski', in *Polish-Anglo Saxon Studies*, vol. I, 41.
2. B. Pares, *History of Russia*, 354.
3. J. Szczepański, *Modernizacja Górnitcwa i Hutnictwa w Królestwie Polskim w i Polowie*, XIX W, 235.
4. FO 392/2 Misc 134.
5. FO 392/4.
6. A. E. Garvie, *Memories and Meanings of My Life*, 32.
7. B Pares, *op cit.*, 410.
8. FO 394/6, Doc 62.
9. J. Szczepański, *op cit.*, 235.
10. A. E. Garvie, *op cit.*, 30–32.
11. Garvie Letters, 1905.

CHAPTER NINE

The Textile Industry

The development of the textile industry in Scotland in the eighteenth century had been spectacular. Woollens were still coarse, quite unable to compete in quality with English cloth, but cotton-spinning was introduced in 1769 and was rapidly mechanised. Factories at Stanley in Perthshire, Catrine and New Lanark on the Clyde – any where accessible to ports and waterpower – employed thousands of spinners who produced yarn for an army of handloom weavers. By the end of the century the most skilled were producing fine fabrics which could rival imports from India. The successful mechanisation of weaving lagged fifty years behind. Early machines caused endless breakages of delicate fibres and in 1838 there were still 51,000 handlooms in use in Scotland. Weaving sheds might house 100 looms but most craftsmen were self-employed and the highly skilled could earn as much, working in their own homes, as the parish minister.

Equally dramatic was the development of linen manufacture. Flax, the raw material, was grown on every sizeable Scottish farm and retted in the retting pool. Spinning the fibres was women's work, supervised by the mistress of the house. The village weaver would turn this thread into cloth good enough for home consumption, and only the gentry would buy fine damask and 'Hollands', imported from the Netherlands. To protect the industry a statute of 1686 ordered that:

> Hereafter no corpse of any person whatever shall be buried in any sheet or anything else except plain linen ... made and spun within the kingdom, without lace or point.

In England a similar act protected the woollen industry and Alexander Pope could write:

> 'Odious! in woollen! 'twould a saint provoke' Were the last words that poor Narscissa spoke.

Because it did not compete with English woollens, linen production

The Old Hand Loom Weaver.

Weaving Leno Curtains
by Handloom in Darvel.

33. Handloom (seen here at Darvel, Ayrshire, Scotland). These complex and expensive handlooms were in use till the second part of the century. Weaving was the last part of the linen textile industry to be mechanised.

was encouraged after the Union of 1707. In 1726 the Board of Trustees for Manufactures made money available to bring skilled artisans from Picardy to train the Edinburgh weavers, and for fifteen years Dutch craftsmen brought over their improved looms and toured the Lowlands, instructing village weavers in their own homes.[1] Industrial espionage abroad was encouraged and prizes were given for improvements in quality and design. The British Linen Bank provided loan capital for a rapidly growing industry. Coarse linen was exported to the West Indies; fine could compete on the home market with the best from Holland. Edward Topham, an observant English visitor to Scotland in 1774, wrote in his *Letters from Edinburgh*:

> The Scotch ... excell the Irish in that species of linen which is calculated for the table; the strength and the beauty of the inter- woven patterns in this article exceed anything the Irish have produced. Formerly the Scotch used to send some of their finest linens to be bleached at Haarlem in Holland; but they found it did not answer the expence of it ... they now bleach it entirely amongst themselves; and as they have good water and good ground I see no reason for sending it from here.[2]

Early attempts to mechanise linen weaving failed; even the spinning process was unsatisfactory until Philippe de Girard invented a machine in 1812 which, after macerating the flax in hot water, could produce a strong fine linen thread. Weaving lagged behind and it was the mid-nineteenth century before power-driven machines replaced the handloom. But by the 1820s poverty was already driving thousands of weavers out of their workshops. Entry into the craft was unprotected by guild regulations, and easily acquired skills, the pleasures of inde- pendent employment and high rates of pay attracted too many young men. Competition for work drove down piece-rates. A strike in 1812 was a complete failure and wages were plummeting long before the cyclical postwar depressions hit British industries. Master craftsmen could still earn a living but, for most men, the drop in average wages from 25/– a week in 1816 to 7/6 in 1830 meant destitution. Thousands emigrated to America; two Scots, James and Thomas Garvie, went to Poland. The Polish textile industry was often dependent on British machines but its skilled workers usually came from Prussia, Saxony and Bohemia. Amongst 50,000 immigrants to the Congress Kingdom the Scottish weavers were insignificant; it was in the second half of the century that the Garvies played a significant part in the development of the linen industry in Poland.

34. Philippe de Girard, 1775–1845. The successful establishment of the linen industry in Poland was based on Girard's inventions and his insistence on quality. Żyrardów was named in his honour.

Profitable textile factories, using wool and flax from their own estates and employing technicians from France and Switzerland, had been set up by Polish landowners in the half-century before the Partitions. Production was disrupted by the French Wars but revived in 1817 when machines were imported from the Cockerill factory in Liège. William Cockerill, an English mechanic working in Belgium, had invented wool-carding and spinning machines in 1799. Unlike the British, the Netherlands government placed no restrictions on the export of machinery, and within a few years his son John had set up another factory in Berlin and a foundry at Seraing in Belgium to meet the demand for the machines. Seven of the new textile factories set up in the Congress Kingdom were equipped with them. These helped to meet the demand for coarse woollen cloth for uniforms for the newly created Polish army. In 1821 Russian and Far Eastern markets were opened to Poles and closed to the Prussians who had previously supplied them. Expanding markets and loans conditional on the introduction of new technologies stimulated the growth of a flourishing woollen industry. With Cockerill's help, a demonstration factory was set up in Warsaw in 1821 and unemployed Prussian workers emigrated to provide a skilled labour force. By 1830 the industry was flourishing and coarse cloth became Poland's main export, representing 82% of the total value of her eastern trade.[3]

Cotton, dependent on imported raw material, was slow to develop. The delegation to Britain in 1825 which was led by Girard and Niepokejczycki was looking for machines and men. The first cotton-spinning mill, opened in 1826, had British machines and James Garvie may have been one of the men recruited to train Polish weavers. Development in cotton was to be in Łódź, 130 kilometres south-west of Warsaw, and Scots do not seem to have played a part in this.[4] Often with German initiative and technicians and British machines it grew slowly, held back as were all Poland's new industries by the hostility of Russian trade policies after 1830. It was 1853 before it could produce even 50% of the demand for cotton thread, and in 1862 only a hundred power looms were in use.[5]

The linen industry had an equally shaky start. General Pac had been developing production in the Augustow region and in 1817 invited a Mr Riach, almost certainly a Scot, to set up a bleach works and factory at Dowspuda.[6] Other improving landowners were doing the same, using flax grown on their own estates. But the Girard factory on the Łubieński estate was the only enterprise planned on a large scale and one of the few private ventures which survived the period between the 1830 Rising and the post-Crimean Thaw. It was to play an increasingly important part in the lives of the Scots in Poland in the late nineteenth century.

Philippe de Girard was an engineer of European standing whose inventive genius was at the centre of the development of Żyrardów. The son of a Waldensian Protestant landowner from Lourmarin in Provence, he had fought as a Girondist against the revolutionaries. Escaping from France on a British warship, he earned a living as a portrait painter in the Balearic Isles and then by manufacturing soap in Livorno and chemicals in a factory near Marseilles. Still in his twenties, he held the Chair of Natural History and Philosophy at the University of Nice. To encourage a branch of the textile industry which used a raw material which could be produced in France, Napoleon offered an award of 8,000 francs to the inventor of a machine which could spin a fine flax thread. Girard had never been inside a textile factory but he shut himself up with a bundle of retted flax fibres and in three days emerged with a blueprint for 'La filature méchanique du Lin'. Investing his own money, he set up two factories in Paris in which his machines produced fine thread. His success was acknowledged in 1813 but he was still waiting for the prize money when Napoleon was defeated. The restored monarchy refused to honour Napoleon's debts and, while Girard was himself in prison for a minor debt, his business partner sold the design of the machine to an English manufacturer. Ten years later, when in London on a mission for the Polish government, he found that 'a Mr Kay' had pirated the invention. Girard successfully challenged his claim to a patent and, in a letter to the *Manchester Guardian* on December 2nd 1826, courteously thanked Mr Kay for drawing the attention of British manufacturers to his invention by the publicity caused by the cancellation of the patent Kay had wrongfully claimed for it.[7]

Girard's contact with the Congress Kingdom had been made in Austria, where he had moved in search of financial backing for his inventions. He had set up a textile factory at Hirtenberg near Vienna and successfully launched the first steam-powered boat to sail up the Danube, but he was still financially insecure. In 1824 Count Łubieński persuaded him to move to Poland where he was appointed Chief Engineer of Mines with a contract which promised an excellent income, a fine house in Warsaw and a life pension. In 1828 he signed another with the newly established 'Société de Filature de Lin' in which he undertook to design and manage a linen factory on the Łubieński estate, 30 kilometres west of Warsaw. The factory which, in honour of Girard, became known as Żyrardów, was planned on ambitious lines. Building started on an impoverished area of the estate at Guzow, and by 1829 the spinning mill and a weaving hall had been built. As at Catrine and New Lanark, accommodation had to be provided for workers and there were five hundred families living on the site by 1830. The factory was to be equipped with machines of Girard's design, some smuggled out from Britain and others to be built by William Preacher in the Białogon factory. Key workers were trained by foreign artisans in a workshop at Ruda and flax-growing was started on the surrounding farms. The opening was seriously delayed by the 1830 Rising but, trading under the name Karol Szoltz & Co, the factory came into production in 1833.

It was the largest in central Europe. Spinning was fully mechanised and powered by a steam engine but the weaving hall held only handlooms. Bleaching and finishing processes were primitive and locally grown flax was of poor quality. More significant was the poor quality of local labour. Recently emancipated peasants were usually illiterate and unskilled, and from the start the management recognised that it would have to attract foreign craftsmen if it were to produce linen of fine quality. Over 25% of the workforce, 150–180 men, came from Bohemia, 8% from Austria and a few from Germany, France, Italy, Hungary and Britain. From Girard's fertile mind came a series of inventions, and during its first ten years the factory was equipped with machines for combing, carding, drawing, bobbing, taping and folding. Between 1833 and 1840 productivity increased 700% and the quality of the linen produced was recognised in 1843 by the first of many Moscow awards.[8]

But the cost of production was enormous. In addition to new machines and factory buildings, the village had to be enlarged to

35.   Żyrardów. The factory *c.* 1840 before its purchase by the Bank Polski in 1848.

36.   The Mill Pond, *c.* 1890. Sandy soil and low winter temperatures made the
supply of water for the factory, and a population of over 30,000, a serious problem.

provide housing for a workforce of over 800. Like so many of the
outstanding figures in the development of the textile industry, Girard
was a Protestant and a paternalist with a real concern for the welfare
of employees. From its initiation, building at Żyrardów had been of
a high standard and housing expensive. The company was in any case
under-capitalised and its finances were further damaged in 1842 by

37. The Fire Brigade, *c.* 1890. Fire risks were high in a textile factory. There were 40 men in the brigade, believed to be the first private fire-fighting force in the Russian Empire.

the Łubieński Affair when the Count, vice-president of the Bank Polski and initiator of the Żyrardów venture, was dismissed. The following year Girard returned to France to receive the recognition that had for so long been withheld. The Gold Medal granted to him at the Paris Exhibition cited ten inventions ranging from textile machines and turbines to musical instruments and hydrostatic lamps: 'Un range très distingué, parmi les inventeurs les plus ingénieux et les plus dignes de participes aux récompense nationales'.[9] He died the following year and never returned to Żyrardów. In 1848 the Bank Polski took over the firm. Productivity plummeted and the workforce was halved. Management by the Bank was so disastrously unsuccessful that when two Bohemian bankers, Karl Hielle and Karl Dittrich, bought the firm at a bargain price in 1857, the income of the factory was little more than 3% of its running costs. By that time the Garvie factory at Sokule had closed down, Thomas Garvie was in charge of the weaving hall at Żyrardów and his son Peter had set up a small factory of his own. Hielle and Dittrich made Thomas a manager, bought up Peter's factory and recruited him into the firm. On Peter's death in 1892 he was succeeded as a director and partner by his son, my grandfather Thomas. Linen production in Poland was to be 'Concentrated in a single plant at Żyrardów where regular investment in new equipment ensured unchallenged predominance in imperial markets'.[10]

NOTES

1. E. Gauldie, *Spinning and Weaving*, 49.
2. E. Topham, *Letters from Edinburgh*, 175.
3. S. Niziol, *British Technology and Polish Economic Development 1815–63*, 64.
4. *Ibid*, 65.
5. *Ibid*, 65.
6. J. Bartyś, 'English and Scottish Farmers in Poland in the first half of the Nineteenth Century', 100, *Agricultural History Review*, Vol. XV, 1967.
7. Girard Archives, Lourmarin.
8. S. Herbsta, *History of Żyrardów, 1830–70* (translation).
9. Girard Archives.
10. S. Niziol, *op cit.*, 105.

CHAPTER TEN

The Garvies

The Garvie brothers were descended from the Macleans of Coll. Backing the wrong side in the first Jacobite Rising of 1689, they forfeited their lands, adopted their nickname 'garbh', the Gaelic for rough or strong, and moved to Perthshire in search of a living. By the end of the eighteenth century Perth had become one of the centres of the developing linen industry and was enjoying a building boom. Peter Garvie was profiting from both. Described as a Wright on his marriage certificate, he was also a weaver at a time when handloom weavers were the aristocrats of Scottish craftsmen. David Bremner, writing in 1869, described them:

> A grave, thoughtful and exceedingly industrious class, and from their ranks went forth many men who took an advanced position in the world of learning and were noted for their commercial enterprise ... men are to be found who possess a knowledge of history, politics and general literature that would adorn a much loftier station in life.[1]

By 1869 there were few survivors amongst these men; as early as 1810 there were too many weavers in Perth and sixty had failed; the postwar depression brought destitution to many more.

At least two of Peter's sons fitted Bremner's description of the enterprising weaver. They had moved to Edinburgh while still young men, James to manage his brother-in-law Gray's textile factory and Thomas to become a master-weaver of Paisley shawls. Copying the designs of shawls brought from Kashmir by the East India Company and selling at £200, skilled weavers in Edinburgh and Norwich in the 1780s, and rather later in Paisley, had been making shawls which could be sold at a profit for £20. The complexity of the designs made it impossible for the unskilled worker to compete with the masters whose earnings remained high. But by the 1820s the Jacquard loom threatened even the best of hand-weavers. Probably recruited by the Polish

116

38. Thomas Garvie, 1852–1918. Thomas was the third generation of Garvies to be involved in the management and direction of the Żyrardów factory.

delegation which toured the industrial areas of Britain in 1825, James decided to emigrate. In the late 1820s he was managing a textile factory at Sokule on the Łubieński estate, west of Warsaw. By 1828 Thomas had joined him, bringing out the capital with which they bought the factory in which James had originally been employed as manager.

James is a shadowy figure who disappears from my mother's memoirs at an early date – 'not', she says, 'a satisfactory character'. The Garvie property at Sokule was damaged in the 1830 Rising and James sued unsuccessfully for compensation in 1834. But he did recover 259.67 roubles, salary owed to him by Prince Ogiński.[2] There is no record of how it had been earned; had he been training Polish weavers at Ruda? About the factory we know more. With a hundred looms of improved design it was producing linen damask. Philippe de Girard was scathing about its quality. In a letter to his niece, written in 1836, he describes it as exhibiting 'in a shocking way' the faults which Girard was trying to eliminate from linen manufactures in the Żyrardów factory.[3] But the Garvie brothers had been able to attract to Sokule some of the skilled workers whom Girard so badly needed. He persuaded Thomas to leave his brother and take charge of the weaving sheds in Żyrardów. The factory was paying James a salary of 7,500 roubles in 1844, the year Girard left Żyrardów. Was James brought in as a consultant? He was still at Sokule in the late 1840s.

Far more is known about Thomas. Born in 1784, he seems, like his Dissenter father, to have been a man to whom religion and literature were important. Of his signed books a seventeenth-century Bible, a hymn book dated Perth 1814, and *Selections from the New Testament for the use of the English Congregation in Poland* and *Orthographical Exercises in Prose and Verse* have survived. One novel came back to Scotland – David Moir's *Mansie Wauch – Tailor in Dalkeith*. In 1824 he married Catherine, the daughter of James Sinclair, a paper-master in Penicuik, where paper-making had been successfully established in the eighteenth century. Catherine never lost touch with her family. First her son Peter and then her grandson Thomas stayed with her brother when sent to Scotland to be educated. My sister, at school in Edinburgh in the 1930s, remembers visiting a very old Sinclair relative still living in the family home in Lauder Road.

It was a Sinclair aunt who carried young Peter to the boat for Danzig when Thomas and his family set out from Leith in 1828. The 350 kilometres from Danzig to Sokule were completed in a canvas-covered postal wagon, an appropriate start for what must have been a very tough life. A few years later the family, with a cow and a bag of meal, was sheltering in the forests from the guns of the 1830 Rising. Thomas emerged from hiding to rejoin his brother at Sokule but by 1833 he was in Żyrardów. The Garvie connection, which was to last till 1918, had been established.[4]

The earliest Garvie letters to have survived date from 1864 but the name appears in consular records from the 1830s onwards. Donations to the Evangelical Reformed Church in Warsaw, requests for passports to visit St Petersburg or London, applications for gun licences and registration of births and marriages are all carefully recorded and add substance to family memoirs.

Peter, the only son, was sent home to Edinburgh to get some technical training. On the certificate of his marriage in 1849 to Jane Kedslie, daughter of Alexander Kedslie the miller, he was a master-weaver. In partnership with Adolph Martin, an Irish bleaching expert, he bought land from Prince Łubieński and set up a small linen textile factory with 116 looms. Spun flax was farmed out to cottage weavers and the cloth finished and marketed by Martin and Garvie. There are no figures by which to measure the success of this venture but at Żyrardów productivity plummeted in the 1850s. The Bank Polski had taken over management in 1848. The workforce had dropped from 800 in 1840 to 400 in 1850 and the venture was on the verge of collapse. An agreement signed by Martin and Garvie with the Bank in 1856 and a payment of 4,600 roubles suggests an attempt to recruit their skills for the weaving and bleaching departments. The sale of the factory to Hielle & Dittrich in 1857 may well have saved Martin and the Garvies, as well as the firm, from financial disaster. They sold looms and their factories to the new owners and became managers in the expanding firm.[5]

With Austrian capital and a loan from the Bank the new owners modernised and mechanised both the bleaching and the weaving processes. Their timing was perfect; railway development in the late 1850s had at last made Russia and the Far East accessible both as a market and a source of good-quality flax. The quality of the linen produced at Zyrardow in Girard's day had been recognised when it won an award at an exhibition at Moscow in 1843. In 1870 Hielle & Dittrich became 'Suppliers to His Majesty the Tsar' and from that date carried the double imperial eagles on their stationery. Productivity and profits soared and the factory, employing over 8,000 people in the 1890s, became the largest textile firm in Russia.[6]

Karl Dittrich was, in his own way, as remarkable a man as Girard. While his partner Hielle seems to have lived most of the time in Austria, Dittrich was more often in Poland and was personally concerned with the development of the firm. A shrewd businessman, he

39. Grand Prix, Paris Exhibition, 1900. Linen produced in Żyrardów was reputed to be the finest in Europe.

was also an idealist and a philanthropist. In the factory the partners set out to manufacture the finest linen in Europe, in Żyrardów to create a model industrial town. They achieved both their objectives. The St Petersburg award was followed by a medal at the Nizny Novgorod exhibition in 1898, the grand prize at the Paris exhibition in 1900 and another imperial award in 1905. My grandmother told us that Żyrardów supplied table linen to Queen Alexandra for Buckingham Palace. 'But not as fine', she said, 'as the linen woven for my trousseau.' Some of this is still in use.

To achieve this quality Hielle and Dittrich realised that they must continue to recruit foreign experts. By 1875 there were Hays, Dicksons and Govenlocks in senior administrative posts; weaving was managed by the Scottish Garvies, bleaching by Antony Cowdy from Belfast and spinning by the Ogdens from Yorkshire. Other familiar names amongst the managerial staff, father often followed by a son, were Shaw, Martin and Reavey. The firm became public in 1885 and by the 1890s there were Garvies, a Govenlock, a Kennedy and Carl Hannich, an Austrian married to a Garvie, on the Board. There were two Polish directors and one Russian but at the end of the century at least 60% of senior personnel were foreigners. Responding to criticism, Dittrich wrote in 1891:

> One must remember that our type of manufacture requires many very well trained specialists. We are the only linen factory in Poland and any experts who are to be trained can only be trained at our factory ... So we have to count on foreigners to fill many of the posts which require special technical training of practical experience ... If we just relied on people trained by us, without new ideas, our factory would just lose ground.[7]

The Garvies fit into this picture. Peter had been sent back to Scotland for engineering training and never lost touch with developments in western Europe. His son's education was wider. Edinburgh Institution had been chosen because it was a school which prepared boys for a life in business or industry rather than for the professions. His final report is worth quoting:

> Thomas Henry Garvie has been a pupil at the Institution for three sessions from October 1865 till July 1868. He has attended classes for English, Elementary Latin, French, German, Arithmetic, Elementary Mathematics, Writing, Book-keeping and Mechanical Drawing. His attendance has been regular, his attention and dilig- ence commendable, his progress very satisfactory and his conduct admirable.
>
> G Nichols
> } Headmasters
> A. M. Ferguson

Twelve of his school prizes, ranging from a first for Religious Instruction to a regrettable ninth for Arithmetic, are now on my study shelves. Returning to Poland, he served an apprenticeship in the factory, spent a year with a French family in Warsaw to improve his French and relearn the Polish he had forgotten, studied business methods in Glasgow and at the firm's headquarters at Schönlinde in Bohemia and, finally, became a student of textiles at the technical college at Chemnitz in Saxony. He took over management of weaving from his father and, on Peter's death in 1892, became a director and then a partner in the firm. On his frequent travels he visited textile factories throughout Europe, probably recruiting personnel for Żyrardów. His own major technical achievement was the patenting of an improved Jacquard loom in 1895, and it is his name which is engraved on the medal presented at the Parish Exhibition in 1900.

The Garvie letters of the 1860s reflect the excitement of the take-off.[8] Thomas never destroyed the letters that had brought him news from home. His father was too busy to write often but there are letters from his sisters and from his Kedslie grandfather Alexander and his aunt Catherine, who looked after the family after his mother's death.

Catherine's letters between 1866 and 1868 often refer to work at the factory:

> Papa is always busy and there is a great deal of movement here. In time Żyrardów will become a manufacturing town ... Papa is well and as usual very busy as they are fitting up a great many new looms ... You will excuse your father writing this time he is more than usually busy. Mr Landman had the misfortune to break his arm and is not able to attend his work which puts your Papa a good deal about as there is enough to do for everyone ... Żyrardów is becoming quite gay.

In 1865 Alexander Kedslie wrote:

> Business here is in a very prosperous state and applications for goods greater than can be supplied. They are enlarging the mills; another story is nearly finished and when all is ready they will produce more than double what they have at present. Your father will I believe have more than five hundred looms ... Mr Ogden [the manager of spinning] is in England for three weeks ...

In the rapidly growing community there were always problems about water and sewage and in 1866 Kedslie wrote:

There have been many deaths from typhus and inflammation, among others old Rerick yesterday. Your father will miss him as he was his best foreman and was expert in errecting the power looms of which in no long time there will be above 500, the houses being ready for them. Although we hear sad accounts from Germany of the want of business here it is not felt where linen goes off as quickly as it can be prepared ... You would hardly know the fabric now it is so enlarged and ornamented ...

A cold wet summer led to a bad harvest:

The potatoes have suffered much from the rot and the prospect for the poor during the winter is one of suffering. In Żyrardów this will not be so much felt because there is abundance of work and good wages and everything that is made meets with an immediate sale.

Kedslie died in 1872. His last surviving letter was addressed to Thomas after his arrival at the technical college at Chemnitz:

Your Father of course keeps you aware of how things are going on here and of the many proposed additions and purposes which fills the brain of Mr Dittrich and seems a necessary of his existence.

One of Dittrich's aims was to create a healthy environment for his workpeople. In a country where housing standards were notoriously low, Girard had employed a Warsaw architect to build a village of substantial cottages, carefully separated from the works. Like David Dale and Robert Owen nearly a hundred years earlier at New Lanark, Dittrich was determined to create a civilised community for the workers. Contemporaries were impressed. In 1868 a reporter for a journal called *Klos* wrote:

Holding to sensible and honourable principles that workers will only be useful to employers in good living conditions and with good pay, the owners of Żyrardów do not save money in their efforts to improve workers' conditions. Daily pay 60–75 kopecks for piece work; clean cheap quarters for permanent staff in 24 buildings provide comfortable accommodation. For casual workers barrack like buildings provide living places; a low charge of 15 kopecks per week entitles workers to a place in a large heated hall, an iron bed with a mattress and free use of a kitchen run by the factory. Medical care and medicine are provided by a hospital fund; two primary and one evening school are free to everyone and a nursery school will shortly open for children whose parents are working most of the day.[9]

By the end of the century there were wash- and bath-houses, a fire brigade, clubs, orchestras and choirs and two Roman Catholic churches. A third church for the largely foreign Protestant congregation was built in the 1890s. Streets of larger houses were built for senior personnel, separated from the rest by their own park. A second park and an 80-bed hospital served the whole community. There were strict rules about drinking and where and when to chop wood, and a curfew was imposed. But long-service employees were given pensions on retirement and there was a residential home for old people. In 1891 Dittrich's son, another Karl, estimated that the cost of social services added approximately 10 roubles to the wages of a worker earning 200 roubles a year. A reporter from a St Petersburg paper described Żyrardów in 1903:

> Żyrardów is like part of the most orderly German province or a Swiss industrial canton. Straight streets and wide hard roadways are separated from comfortable pavements by deep stone gutters. Houses are usually of red brick, well built and nice looking. Everything is clean and pleasing to the eye and everywhere there is greenery.[10]

The Garvies shared Dittrich's concern for the welfare of the workers and were probably equally paternalistic and authoritarian in their outlook. Peter had been born in his mother's home in Penicuik, where Cowan's paperworks were the main employers. Writing about conditions in the factory there, Bremner wrote in 1868:

> The wives and daughters of the partners have always taken a special interest in the sick, and since 1823 have managed a school for the education of the children of the workpeople. In 1840 a commodious school-house was built near the mills ... The young persons engaged in the mills are compelled to attend free evening

40. Elizabeth Garvie (née Dickson), 1860–1954. Elizabeth and her daughters, Jean and Elizabeth, *c.* 1890. A farmer's daughter, she identified with Poland and never felt at home in Britain.

41. Jean and Peter Garvie, *c.* 1896. Their father brought the children up to think of Scotland as their home.

classes during three months in the winter season ... About 30 years ago the following rules were put in force by Messers Cowan: 1. No child under 13 years of age shall be employed. 2. No young persons shall be employed before they are able to read, write and figure and, in the case of girls, to sew. 3. Wives shall not be employed as it is considered that they should be 'keepers at home' for the sake of their husbands and children.[11]

To put this and Żyrardów in perspective, conditions should be compared with those in St Petersburg factories at the turn of the century. Semen Kanatchikov, son of an emancipated serf, served an apprenticeship in a metal factory in the 1890s. In *A People's Tragedy* O Figes quotes from the memoirs he wrote many years later:

Many workers had to make do with a narrow plank bed in the factory barracks where hundreds of men, women and children slept together in rows with nothing but their own dirty clothes for bedding. In these barracks which Gorky compares with "dwellings of a prehistoric people", there were neither washing nor cooking facilites so the workers had to visit the bath house and eat in canteens. There were whole families living in these conditions. They tried as best they could to get a little privacy by hanging a curtain around their plank-beds. Others, even less fortunate, were forced to live in the flop-house and eat and sleep by the side of their machines. Such was the demand for accommodation that workers thought nothing of spending half their income on rent ... Sixteen people lived in the average apartment in St Petersburg, six in every room according to a survey of 1904 ...[12]

The Garvies were brought up in the Cowan tradition. Trade unions were illegal in the Russian empire and laws to protect vulnerable employees easily evaded. At Żyrardów the directors believed that the welfare of the workforce was the responsibility of management and were proud of their record. When the cholera epidemic which swept across Europe in the 1860s reached Żyrardów in 1864, the factory provided boiled drinking water for the community. In his autobiography Peter's son Alfred described the scene:

In their ignorance and fatalism many of the people disregarded all precautions and death entered into most of the homes. A mark was made on the door where a corpse was. Such was the dread that the working man refused to perform the service of burial until my father and other heads of the business shamed them by setting them an example.[13]

Until stopped by the Russian authorities, Peter's daughters ran a Sunday school and other members of the family circle, Hays, Dicksons and Govenlocks, were closely connected with the development of schools and of the 80-bed hospital. Janet Dickson, one of its early matrons, was reputed to have known everybody in Żyrardów and to have nursed many of its most accomplished thieves – 'So clever', she said, 'that they could steal from the gipsies'. When the Germans, during the First World War, stole valuable equipment and drugs from the hospital, she employed the thieves who had become her friends to get them back.

Thomas was a man of similar calibre. He persuaded his fellow directors to open what had been their private park to the whole community and, in the workers' park, made sure that there was an area where nursing mothers could have privacy to feed their babies. During the 1905 Revolution his children were sent to England for safety. To reassure them, he and my grandmother Elizabeth wrote several times a week during periods when reports reaching Britain were particularly alarming. The tone of their letters was always sympathetic to the workers. In March Elizabeth wrote:

> The factory is not working apart from the stocking and bleaching divisions and these two sections are to be stopped on Thursday. The silence is not pleasant. People are splendid but the misery must be terrible.[14]

Thomas believed that strikers were the prey of professional agitators. Ten days later he wrote:

> ... The strike is now at an end and our people are working since Tuesday morning ... As far as we can hear there is not the slightest wish among them to cause any disturbance, so there is

42. Żyrardów. The directors' houses were in a street near the park. The Garvies' (*centre*) was big enough to provide a refuge for relations and Scottish friends.

every hope that we shall not be affected by the movement in Łódź and elsewhere.

When Germany and Austria went to war with Russia in 1914 the imperial government confiscated the Żyrardów factory and started to move its valuable machinery to Russia. Thomas came out of semi-retirement in Scotland to rescue the firm and its employees. In January 1915 he wrote to his daughter Jean from Copenhagen:

I am returning to Petrograd and from there going on via Moscow to Warsaw where I shall have a good deal to do in connection with our works which as you know have been standing since beginning of October. Although we are not working we are allowing all of our work people a small sum weekly to help them to live: we have also arranged a public soup kitchen in which about 3,500 meals are distributed every day.

When the Germans reoccupied Poland, he retreated to Moscow and spent the rest of the war – and his life – trying to salvage what was left of the company's property. He died alone in Murmansk in 1918.

When his father Peter died in 1892, the workpeople paid for a mass for the comfort of his family and asked that the funeral be postponed till a Sunday so that they could follow his coffin to the grave. Authoritarian and paternalistic they might be, but they were respected and loved by many of their employees. They shared Dittrich's attitudes and ambitions and must have made a major contribution to the development of his model industrial town.

NOTES

1. D. Bremner, *The Industries of Scotland*, 166.
2. Foreign Office 39312 Mis 11.
3. Girard Archives.
4. A. E. Garvie, *Memories and Meanings of my Life*, 29.
5. A Stawarz, *Żyrardów Narodziny Spolecznosci*.
6. A. Herbsta, *Historja Żyrardów 1830–70*.
7. K. Dittrich, Report on the Strike at Żyrardów 1891.
8. Garvie Letters.
9. S. Herbsta, *op cit*.
10. *Ibid*.
11. D. Bremner, *op cit.*, 335.
12. O. Figes, *A People's Tragedy*, 111.
13. A. E. Garvie, *op cit.*, 25.
14. Garvie Letters.

CHAPTER ELEVEN

The Scottish Circle

The thousands of Scots who lived in Poland in the seventeenth century were part of an organised community. Brotherhoods which existed in towns like Lublin and Cracow collected taxes from their members to finance the provision of schools, hospitals and churches and the care of widows and orphans. By the end of the eighteenth century there were some Scottish names in Poland but few unpolonised Scots. The Brotherhoods had been dissolved and there were no societies waiting to welcome the first of the immigrants to Poland in the early nineteenth century.

The earliest of these, the engineers and technicians who worked with John Macdonald at Zwierzyniec in south-east Poland, must have formed a tightly knit group, united by language and their Protestant faith. For several generations the Zamoyskis had been anglophiles with strong Scottish links but the social gap between the immigrants and their employers would have been unbridgeable. The names of the settlers appear as witnesses on marriage and christening certificates and their children seem to have stayed on in Poland, but I have found no record of their personal experiences. Many of the settlers on the Dowspuda estate, however, were related to my mother. From some of the books they took out to Poland, which came back nearly a hundred years later, and from a few surviving letters it is possible to imagine how they lived.

The postal system was primitive, slow and expensive. It was 1840 before the penny post was introduced in Britain and 1860 before there was a pre-paid system in Poland. Early letters to William Hay are on one sheet of paper, written and counter-written by his father and sisters, folded, sealed and addressed to 'Mr Hay, c/o Mr Blaikie at Dospuda Poland'. In transit across the Continent, 'Per Hamburg, Konongsburg et Olezko' have been added. A letter written by James to his father on July 1st 1824 reached Scotland at the end of October but neither it nor any of his other letters has survived. A picture of life amongst the five hundred or so Scots on General Pac's estates can only be built up from his sisters' responses to William's descriptions of life in Poland, and William was clearly no letter writer. In 1824 his father wrote: 'We were much disturbed being so very long in not hearing from you', and in 1841 his sister Beatrix's letter started 'Although you have never answered the long letter I wrote you this time last year ...' [1]

The picture which emerges is of a community with an English-speaking hierarchy. In 1824 William was living with or near a Captain and Mrs de Lacy, and his father wrote:

> It is a lucky circumstance that you are with a family of British lineage and language ...

In the same letter Beatrix added:

> I rejoice greatly to hear that your children are such favourites with Mrs de lacy, it is particularly lucky on Jean's account, as it will be the means of grounding her well in English.

Jean had been born after her parents' arrival in Poland in 1818 and the problems of language and the education of their children must have been serious for all the immigrants. Janet Hay was worried because her nephews and nieces could neither read nor write English and by 1834 was writing to her brother:

> You seem to have forgot your English very much the most common words are wrong spelled. When you write Mr Stuart [the family's Edinburgh lawyer] use your dictionary.

There are no references to schools. The first generation of Scots born in Poland were probably educated at home, and letters from the Hay sisters are full of good advice. In 1834 Janet wrote:

> They ought to get their German language it is more generally in use than Polish, it may prove very useful; education is much attended to in this country and carried on in a different way than formerly; the children are now made to understand what they read and their attention and observation brought forward to every-thing about them that is worthy of note, and the poorest children

43. The Protestant Church, Suwałki. Settlers on the Dowspuda estate worshipped here, separated by their Protestantism from predominantly Catholic neighbours.

are taught in the same way. You mention the great preparations for Easter, could your boys tell me at once what is the meaning of that, or were I to question them about your neighbour the Stork, what food it eats etc. or about the Jews? You have got Robinson Crusoe that is a nice book for them, what is a Desert? an Island? a Continent? and so on would be some of the questions put; Arithmetic and Geography and the modern languages are thought more useful than Greek and Latin. English Grammar is now taught in almost every little school – the above is hints for winter evenings.

Reading must have been one of the few entertainments during the winter and attendance at the Protestant church at Suwałki one of the few social events of the week. The more isolated families probably held their own services. William Hay's son James was a strict sabbatarian who would not allow horses to be harnessed on a Sunday. His household would almost certainly have observed the Scottish Sabbath as described by Alfred Garvie many years later:

> We took no part in the social gatherings of the day; there might be an enlarged family gathering with some intimate friends but the only amusement was a sedate walk in the summer in a wood near by. My father conducted a short service in the morning and we children had to learn some verses of metrical psalm or hymn, a portion of Scripture and some answers from the Shorter Catechism.[2]

Several family bibles and hymn books have survived and over a hundred books. Alexander Kedslie is described by his daughter as being 'as fond as ever of his books and newspapers', and of the Garvie household she wrote: 'We have always plenty of nice books and we feal quite happy when we can sit down to read together'. A lot of books in German came back in 1906 and a few in French, Polish and Russian. Warsaw bookshops must have been well stocked.

Unlike the German farmers, settlers on the Dowspuda estate do not seem to have been heavy drinkers. In their leases brewing or distilling on their own farms was prohibited. Clause Seven in the contract signed by William Hay in 1821 reads:

The tenant binds himself and foresaids not to erect or carry any distillery or brewery on the said lands as also to carry no vodka or whiskey or malt liquor to his own or any other house, except that found in the public houses in the said Earldom.[3]

But the practice the Scots introduced of chasing spirits with beer still exists in north-east Poland.

By the 1840s most of the younger generation had moved south and were marrying into the very different community around Warsaw. Its centre was the Evangelical Reformed Church where services might be in German, Polish, Czech, French or English. The consul recorded contributions to church funds. In the 1840s there were usually donations from sixteen or seventeen of my mother's relatives, Alexander Kedslie heading the list with 60 roubles each year and James Hay, William's son, closing it with 12. During the Crimean War the community was shaken by the insecurity of its position. In 1855 Miss Kedslie and Miss Broomfield, both employed as companions to members of the Polish aristocracy, were the only contributors. The total dropped from 381.10 roubles to 1.75.[4] Recovery was very slow and some names – Alexander Kedslie's for example – disappeared. Was he in financial difficulties or, having moved in retirement to his daughter's house in Żyrardów, did he contribute to the Protestant meeting house there?

The Warsaw circle was less Scottish and more cosmopolitan than the Dowspuda one. Its members had had to master German and Russian as well as Polish and many had close contacts with their employers, usually members of the French-speaking aristocracy. Most of the Scots who moved from the north-east in the 1830s continued to farm but were drawn into the more sophisticated Warsaw society. William Hay's letters, after he left the Dowspuda estate, were addressed 'c/o D Evans' – the Welsh engineer – and then 'c/o Lilpop and Rau', the Poles they had trained who took over the firm from the Evans brothers after the Crimean War. The circle was widened by marriages with Protestants outside the Scottish community. The Italian architects, the Marconis, married into both Scottish and English families. Two of the Garvie girls married Germans and the first Polish husband, a Mr Oswianki, crept into the family, perhaps by the back door. His wife, Elizabeth, John Dickson's youngest daughter, disappears from the

44. Life in the Country. Both the Hays and the Dicksons had stud farms and a
reputation for fine horsemanship.

45. Life in the Country. Elizabeth Dickson (née Hay) at Strzyzew, the Garvies' country estate, with some of her family, *c.* 1885. Her son-in-law Thomas Garvie and her daughter Elizabeth are on her left.

family's memoirs but, as a wrongdoer, she made her mark in consular papers.

It is easier to trace the careers of the successful members of the Scottish circle than of its failures. Most of the descendants of the original immigrants were absorbed into Polish society and have been forgotten, but the criminals and the sinners have been recorded. In 1864 Elizabeth applied for a passport for her son William. His birth had been registered in November 1839. Her declaration reads:

> I, Elizabeth Oswianka formerly Dickson, British subject living at Leonkowska Niska, declare that William Dickson, living with me at said Leonkowska Niska is my son, begotten of vice, born March 1839. I was unmarried, and to the best of my knowledge he has not by act or deed forfeited rights and privileges of a British subject.[5]

The passport was granted but this is almost certainly the William Hay who was expelled in 1866 for the part he had played in the 1863

Rising. Mr Oswianki was probably persuaded to marry Elizabeth to give her and her illegitimate son a home.

Twenty years earlier one of the Douglas family had been in trouble. Writing from prison in Lublin, Andrew Douglas complained that his health was being impaired and asked the consul to plead for a reduction of sentence. In June 1846 he wrote:

> Having lately had the opportunity of seeing Mr Neil he told me that Mr Kedslie had said to him that he would try to get me set at liberty.[6]

There seem to have been two Andrews in the Douglas family; was this the 'machine constructor' who was sentenced to four years' hard labour for assaulting William Ferguson while working on his farm at Biszcza?[7]

The only scandal recorded in my own family memoirs involved the consul of the time, Colonel Maud. Henry Hay was one of the third generation of Scots in Poland, the third of James Hay's sons. Perhaps significantly, 'he did not complete his studies at the Warsaw Gymnasium' but was sent to Germany to train as a farmer. He became manager of the consul's estate and was implicated in a gambling scandal in which he may have been used as a cover for Colonel Maud. Disgraced in the eyes of the community, he emigrated to Australia where he disappeared, leaving a French wife and two sons, who knew nothing of his origins, behind him. One of these, when studying electrical engineering many years later, came across a textbook by Albert Hay, Henry's brother, and by writing to him recovered his links with Poland.[8] Australia seems to have been the family's favourite dumping-ground for black sheep. In 1868 Alexander wrote to his grandson:[9]

> My nephew John Kedslie has turned out (as I had feared) a worthless vagabond and is a railway porter in Australia and a confirmed drunkard. He must have run through £5 or £6,000.[10]

By the second half of the century an educational pattern had been established amongst the more successful. Daughters were taught at home by relatives or a governess and were expected to become fluent in four or five languages. Several had 'positions' in aristocratic families. Peter Garvie's sister Margaret was in London with Countess Potocki

46. Life in the Country. Jean and Peter Garvie at Strzyzew *c.* 1898.

in 1847 and Agnes Stevenson and Agnes and Catherine Kedslie were all employed as companions to 'young ladies' who seemed to spend winters in their town houses in Warsaw and summers in their own or their relatives' homes in the country. In August 1865 Jane Garvie wrote to her son:

> Aunt Aggy has been here for three weeks as her young lady went to see her sister at Lublin so she allowed Aunty to come here while she was away but she is returned to Warsaw last week.

Marriage, or housekeeping for a bachelor brother, were the only acceptable alternative occupations. It was the end of the century before some of the girls in the Scottish families trained as nurses or were sent back to Britain for higher education. In 1865 Catherine Kedslie was reluctantly released by her employer to look after the Żyrardów household after the death of her sister Jane. Agnes Kedslie remained in employment till retirement. To her nephew Thomas Catherine wrote:

> The situation that Aunt Agnes is in is very gay. She goes a great deal into Society which does not suit her taste or inclination.

Aunt Agnes seems to have been far from gay. She plagued the lives of her nephews and nieces when she joined them when they were at school in Edinburgh in the 1870s.

Boys in the prosperous families were often sent to gymnasium in Warsaw. The less able usually became farmers – the academically gifted 'completed their studies' and went on to university or technical college. James Hay, himself a successful farmer, had eight sons. Of these Alfred, Edmond and Leopold were sent to Edinburgh or Glasgow Universities, William to Dorpat University in Russia 'where he did not work' and then to Warsaw where his father could keep an eye on him. Thomas was sent to a commercial college in Leipzig and Albert to one in Warsaw. Henry and Peter trained as farmers. Some of the brightest never came back to Poland. Alfred became a professor of electrical engineering in England and then principal of the Indian Institute of Science at Bangalore, Edmond had a successful career as a doctor in London, and Leopold went from Edinburgh to Guelph in Canada where he graduated and practised as a vet. Of those who were educated nearer home, William advised Dittrich on the design of the hospital

47. Warsaw: Teatr Wielki, 1833. Warsaw, with its theatre, concert halls, restaurants and bookshops, was the social centre for the community of Scots who were financially successful.

48. Warsaw: the Evangelical Reformed Church. The Scots wre making substantial contributions to the finances of the church by mid-century. There were still Govenlocks and Machlejds (McLeods) in the congregation in 1998.

of which he became the first superintendent, and Thomas was a director of the Karma-Volga Bank in Russia. Albert had a long career as a failed businessman, bailed out from disaster after disaster by his cousin and brother-in-law Thomas Garvie. Peter became a farmer and horse breeder and Henry the manager of the consul's estate. Both Alexander Kedslie's sons re-emigrated to Canada and graduated at Toronto University, while Alexander Watson's son went to India. Opportunities for the ambitious and able seem to have been limited in Poland. With British passports, careers in Britain or the Empire may have seemed more promising than in the Russian territories.

Two passports which have survived suggest that, by the end of the century, successful farmers could afford to travel. John Dickson had been described as 'an honest ploughman' when he came out to Poland in 1820. In the 1830s he was referred to by Stanisław Zamoyski as 'an exemplary farmer and cattle breeder'. By 1881 his son Thomas's wife, Elizabeth Hay, was able to travel extensively with her three daughters. Her passport was issued in Warsaw by the Consul General, Colonel Maude, and stamped seven times by Russian officials before she was issued with a new one in 1896. This was signed by the Lord Provost of Edinburgh. Although her home was still in Poland, she was described as 'Mrs Elizabeth Dickson of Edinburgh a British subject'.

The same picture of middle-class affluence is created by the marriage contract signed in 1881 by her son William and Agnes Garvie. Two copies, one in Russian and the other in Polish, were drawn up by a Warsaw lawyer. William was to bring 9,000 roubles to the marriage and Agnes 8,000, plus furniture and linen to the value of 3,000. Each would retain full possession of the capital they had provided but earnings were to be shared. At the time of their marriage William had his own farm and was manager of the Strzyzew estate.

Most of the farmers who stayed in Poland were successful. They appear in consular records in requests for licences to keep guns and are referred to as 'possessors' of their farms and estates rather than tenants. In faded sepia photos they are mounted on fine horses or pose after a shoot in the forest. The hunting trophies which came back to Scotland in 1906 still delight my grandchildren. Farmhouses are sprawling wooden bungalows; manor houses are more often brick-built and porticoed, with two storeys over the storage cellars.

Family parties are usually formally dressed, seated on a wooden verandah or gathered round a samovar on a cloth-covered table in a heavily furnished room. There would still be English books on the shelves and *The Illustrated London News*, and other journals subscribed to by the wealthier families may have circulated amongst some of the Scots. But the language of the kitchen and the fields was Polish. Amongst my mother's relatives, the Garvies, the Hays and the Kedslies were probably the only families who were reading Gibbon's *Decline and Fall* and the novels of Dickens and George Eliot as well as the Waverley Novels and poetry. By the third generation, farming families like the Dicksons were becoming increasingly polonised, and by 1900 many of my mother's cousins were writing messages in her autograph book in Polish, not English. The novels on my grandmother's bed table were more likely to be in Russian than English.

NOTES

1. Hay Letters, 1818–70.
2. A. E. Garvie, *Memories and Meanings of My Life*, 54.
3. National Archives, Suwałki, 1815–21.
4. FO 394, 65/346.
5. FO 394/6 D62.
6. FO 392/2 Mis 95.
7. S. Niziol, *British Technology and Polish Economic Development*.
8. Hay Memoirs.
9. Garvie Letters, 1864–72.
10. *Ibid.*

CHAPTER TWELVE

Żyrardów

Of his childhood in Żyrardów my grand-uncle A. E. Garvie wrote:

> Although most of the Scottish families who settled in Poland
> became assimilated to their environment, ceased to speak English
> and adopted the customs and even prejudices of the country,
> retaining however their British nationality and Protestant religion,
> my home was an exception ... The surroundings in Żyrardów
> were more cosmopolitan than distinctively Polish.[1]

The Hays and the Dicksons were drawn back into this wider world
by marriage. My grandmother, Elizabeth Dickson, though by blood a
pure Scot, grew up in a family which was identifying with its Polish
neighbours. It was only when she married a Garvie that she came into
a society which had remained stubbornly Scottish and was to become
increasingly cosmopolitan.

49. Directors and Senior Managers, 1888. Very few of these were Poles. Thomas
Garvie is third from the right, front row.

50. The Orchestra. The Ballroom in the Club was used for concerts and dances.

Żyrardów had become a small industrial town before the end of the century, although still officially a village till 1916. By the 1890s nearly a third of its 32,000 inhabitants were employed in the textile factory.[2] With Garvies as directors and partners and over half the senior management foreign, employment by Hielle & Dittrich must have been an attractive and possible alternative to work on the family farm for descendants of the early settlers. By the early 1870s there were Scots, Irish and English as well as Austrians, Czechs and Germans amongst the employees, and a Scot would have moved into a ready-made circle of friends and relations. Peter Govenlock, whose grandfather had been a shepherd in the Scottish Borders, became a director. There were Kennedys and Martins in senior management, one of the Garvie aunts was in the Counting House, and a Hay was employed in Russia as an agent for the firm. Govenlocks and Dick-sons were involved in the development of the hospital of which Dr William Hay became the superintendent and his cousin Janet Dickson the matron. But being a Scot did not guarantee anyone a job. In a letter to her son in 1864 Jane Garvie wrote:[3]

Mr Laing did not get a place here as he quarrelled with Mr Ogden [the Yorkshire manager of the spinning mill] so he would not agree to let Mr Dittrich engage him, so the Laings are very badly off as he has got no other place.

Some months later Mrs Laing and her daughters were staying with the Garvies whose home was one of the houses, large and substantial by Polish standards, which the firm had built for senior personnel. It seems to have become a refuge for Scots in trouble.

The factory created its own social life. There was a club with accommodation for important visitors and a ballroom for concerts and dances. In January 1865 Jane wrote:

There is to be a Ball here in three weeks time. The Gesang Verein [choral society] is giving it for the benefit of the poor so everyone is to pay for their ticket whatever they like and as only genteel people are to be at it they expect to gather a good deal. They have sent an invitation to all the Sugar Factories [the only other industry in the district] and to the gentry and it is to be held in the large room of the Foscal.

In February she continued the story:

The frost has been so severe that for the last fortnight it has been from 20 to 15 degrees of Reumar and when we were coming home from the Ball we thought we would be frozen. There was about 150 people there and they danced a good deal ... and the singing went off pretty well.

Forty years later Thomas was writing to his daughter Jean:

On Saturday there is to be a costume ball for the Gesang Verein and Mama is preparing a costume for it: it is to be kept a secret from me so I do not know what it is to be ...

In the summer there would be picnics in the forest – 'There was a Kirchengesangverein [Church choral society] picnic in the woods and a concert at Ruda' – and all the year round the entertaining of family, friends and business contacts. In 1902 Thomas Garvie wrote:

Mr Farrel from Belfast will likely have dinner with us to-day so

51. The Choir. In the summer concerts were sometimes given in the woods.

it will be necessary to ask Cowdy and Kennedy [the managers of the dyeing and weaving departments] to come too and a better dinner must be arranged. Hanna [the cook] must see what she can get ready.

Warsaw, at last connected by rail to Żyrardów, provided shops, theatres and, through the church, links with the largely foreign protestant community. Major Murray, the British consul, became a close family friend. During the 1905 Revolution my grandmother wrote:

> On Wednesday the Consul was here, humorous as usual but his hearing is worse. Now, without his ear trumpet, he can scarcely hear. He arrived at 12.30 and left at 8.30 pm. He was very grateful for his reception and said it was his first pleasant and quiet day for weeks.

His wife never recovered from post–natal depression. Their only son, Sandy, spent many of his holidays with the Garvies at Strzyzew and travelled with them to England when he was sent to the naval college at Dartmouth and Peter to Mill Hill School. They were both killed during the Great War. The ikon which Major Murray gave to my grandmother in his memory is still in the family.

Holidays loom large in the surviving letters: Ciechocinek, Zakopane and innumerable German 'Bads' to improve their health; Venice, Prague and the Italian Lakes purely for pleasure. And every journey to Britain on business would be followed by as many days as could be spared to visit Scottish relatives and to tour the Highlands. Dittrich insisted that, if he were not there himself, there should always be at least one of the senior executive directors in residence in Żyrardów. Garvie frequently had to cut short his holidays, leaving his wife and children in Britain while he returned to Poland.

Educational opportunities were improving in Poland in the second half of the century, but the wealthier Scots increasingly educated their children privately. In the 1860s the Garvie children were still attending a primary school in Żyrardów, where teaching was in German and most of the children came from managerial homes. A second school was for the Polish-speaking community from the factory. In 1864 nine-year-old Alice wrote to her brother: 'We are all in a great stir in the School because we are expecting the Inspector'. By contemporary standards the school was well staffed. In 1820 the Royal High School in Edinburgh had five graduate masters for 800 boys; at Żyrardów there were 31 teachers for 1,000 pupils.[4] But two years later all their lessons seem to have been at home. Alice described their day:

> Our time is very much taken up now; first in the morning we take lessons from a bore – she is called Miss Schaffer she teaches in Russian, German and Polish, we likewise take lessons from Aunty Katie and Mr Steinke [a master from the factory school] and music from a clarke here, so you must know that we must take it in the evening. Papa learns French from Aunt Cathy and Aunt Maggie also learns music with us.

Fortunately Miss Schaffer did not last long and less than a year later Aunt Katie wrote:

> Miss Schaffer left us about a month ago so we have more room and feel more at ease alone and now Mr Steinke comes regularly three times a week.

In the 1870s Peter Garvie rented a flat in Edinburgh so that the three youngest children and one of their cousins could go to school there, the boys to George Watson's College and the girls to the Merchant Maidens'. Both boys went on to Edinburgh University and Alfred to Glasgow and Oxford. Alfred became a distinguished theologian; and his cousin Charles, to quote from my mother's memoirs, 'a brilliant engineer who drank himself to death'.

My mother and most of her cousins were sent to a Warsaw boarding school where pupils were usually the daughters of minor Polish landowners. When she was seventeen an English governess, a Miss Bennett, was being employed to coach her for matriculation at Westfield College, London. Mr Roberts, the tutor who was preparing her ten-year-old brother for an English public school, had a tougher assignment. In February 1904 his father wrote:

> Peter is getting on pretty well with his tutor, there are however small storms as Peter has not yet got accustomed to obey his teacher and there is some difficulty in learning this lesson.

During his childhood his mother and the servants would have spoken to him in Polish, his father and many of the family friends in English and his early education would have been in German. On the outbreak of the 1905 Revolution he was sent to England before Mr Roberts had had time to make much impact on his written English. Early postcards to his sister from Mill Hill School were in Polish; in his first surviving letter in English there were three alternative spellings of 'jam'. He asked for 'tined apricots' and 'hunny' to be sent from home and he hoped that his letter would not be 'over-wayt'. The mastery of multiple languages presented a serious problem for the less academically able and, in Peter's case, may have led to the development of a stammer. But he was good at maths and, with patient and wealthy parents behind him – 'Poor Peter, he again didn't pass but he can continue and at last, in the second year, or when he wants, he will pass', wrote his mother – he eventually qualified as an engineer at the Royal Technical College, Glasgow. At the University my mother added Gaelic to the five languages she already spoke. Seven of her girl cousins qualified professionally in England but, by the twentieth century, the trickle of returning Scots had become a flood and they were all in Britain with their parents.

52. The Hospital, 1995. This was designed by Karl Dittrich and Dr William Hay.
Like most of the buildings in Zyradów, it was built with bricks from the firm's brick
factory.

While members of the Żyrardów circle were strengthening their Scottish connections, farming relatives and the time they spent on their own estates kept them in close touch with Polish traditions. To escape from the noise of the factory and the smells of the open drains in the town, children were usually sent to the country during school holidays and were looked after by relations. In the summer, days were spent riding, swimming and fishing, and in the winter, skating and sledging. Here Peter was in his element: 'The skating is splendid. Mr Roberts and Peter are out on the ice at least a couple of hours every day'. Some years earlier his mother had written:

> Peter would like to spend day and night on his new horse. He has been fishing with a net but not very successfully, he comes in wet and dirty. Papa is meeting with Baekman [one of the German directors].

Papa rarely had time at Strzyzew. My grandmother's letter of July 1895 describes a recurring situation:

> Ask Aunty Jania to send the passports, Grannie's, yours, Peter's and mine, they must be sent to Warsaw before we go abroad … Papa is a good deal tormented with things in the factory and as Mr Dittrich is not here and nobody knows when he is coming, so most likely we will be obliged to go alone.

Ten years later my mother described escaping from her grandmother's care to visit the village of Sochaczew, not far from Chopin's birthplace. To her brother, desperately homesick at Mill Hill, she wrote:

> Another day we drove to see Sochczew as Tom [a Dickson cousin] wished to go with us but we knew Granny would not let us go without Michael [the coachman] so while she went out to the garden we had to escape along the river, through some potatoes cabbages and rasberries and through a hole in the paling and into the courtyard, Tom acting as guide all the time. In the yard we packed ourselves into the bryczka [a light carriage]; it was a jolly tight fit. We drove very recklessly with Tom's mare and Sirka lazy creature [Peter's pony] did not draw. We saw

Sochaczew went to the ruins of the Castle to the Church the Synagogue theatre and the hospital. The drive back was far more exciting ... It got quite dark the roads were awful and we drove as fast as we could ...

Unfortunately the rest of the letter is missing and we never find out what Granny said when they got home.

In lectures given many years later, my mother described the peasants' customs of the 1890s, their villages, courtship and marriage ceremonies and the celebration of Christmas and Easter. The fast supper on Christmas Eve — as many as twelve fish dishes before the poppyseed cakes and dried fruit compôte — was followed by midnight mass for the Catholic servants. On Christmas morning mummers went from house to house. In her lecture notes she wrote:

> There always was a Herod, Death and the Devil. From the safe perch of my grandfather's shoulder I watched, fascinated, the antics of white-robed Death as it danced round Herod and waved its long scythe. The Devil wasn't nearly as interesting or terrible to me. He was in black, in a short German coat — he used many German words and phrases that, according to an old Polish tradition, being his native language.[5]

The devil may have been wearing a German coat but Germans and German culture played an important part in Żyrardów society. Peter Garvie owned all the works of Schiller and Goethe as well as a magnificent two-volume Bible, Luther's translation illustrated by Gustaf Doré. Board meetings were increasingly held in Berlin and German was the language of business. Peter's closest friend was a Mr Watrobski, one of the two Polish directors, but he was an exception. The names which occur frequently in correspondence suggest that the Scots were part of the social circle formed by a predominantly German-speaking group of foreign directors and managers. Many of them attended the church built by Dittrich for the Protestant community and were buried alongside the Germans in the graveyard at Wiskitki, a few miles from the town. The younger generation had already been separated by the two-school system; Alfred Garvie said that, as a child, he had no Polish friends. Nine-year-old Agnes wrote to her brother Thomas:

53. Dr William Hay, 1853–1901. Dr Hay was on the staff of the firm and became
the first superintendent of the Hospital.

We all look forward to the approach of spring and summer there is such a pretty green turf and so many pretty flowers in the garden, that we never feel inclined to go any where else in search of amusement. It is also surrounded by a good paling so no strange children can get in.

My grandmother gave annual 'Polish Suppers' but these were special occasions at which she would have been more at ease than her husband. In February 1904 he wrote:

Last night we had our annual Polish supper. There were altogether 28 persons present. All the places were taken up, the party was a success and our visitors apparently enjoyed themselves.

The 'grand Kaffe Clatch' she gave a few days later sounds more like a German occasion. 'There are to be fourteen ladies so there will be a good deal of talking.' Integration with the Polish middle classes was still being delayed by religious differences, and it was with Austrians and Germans that the links were becoming closer. Cards announcing my mother's engagement in 1912 were in English and German and, when visiting relatives in the 1920s, Alfred found that the only language they all spoke fluently was German.

The Żyrardów Scots made contact with Poles mainly when employing them. Though staunchly Presbyterian, the Garvies were no bigots and respected the beliefs of others. Alfred, who was to become a leader of the European ecumenical movement, described their servants as being equally ignorant and superstitious whether they were Protestant or Catholic. A maid of German Lutheran descent is reported to have said:

I don't know much about it, but I think my father told me that the Catholics worship a woman Mary and we a man Martin.

The string of abusive terms hurled at the maid by a virago of a Catholic cook reached its climax with 'Luther, Calvin, Garibaldi', Garibaldi being seen as the instrument of the Devil as his army entered Rome. There were no Jews employed by Hielle & Dittrich but Jews often owned the shops and cafés in the town. A butcher from a neighbouring village used to sell meat outside the gates during the factory breakfast hour and had to leave home too early to say his prayers. Aunt Katie, who ran the Garvie household, provided him with a room in which he had privacy to don his prayer shawl after he had finished his business. A particularly devout Catholic gardener, who was allowed to decorate and use an underground winter potato store as a chapel when it was empty in the summer, was indignant when young Alfred told him that 'The Mother of God' was a Jewess. He claimed that everyone knew that she was Polish and came from Częstochowa, the home of the Black Madonna. He was equally indignant when his habit of taking produce from the garden and selling it was challenged. 'It would be strange if, working in such a garden, I could not have a bit of vegetable for my Sunday dinner.' Theft seems to have been normal and acceptable. A maid found stealing from the pantry held out her hands and said, 'The Lord God gave hands. What for?'[6] In spite of this, my grandmother continued to recruit her cooks and housemaids from Poland long after the family had returned to Britain. A few brushes with English servants persuaded her to stick to the devils she knew. And one of her Catholic maids had endeared herself to the family when she was overheard praying, 'Pity the family with whom I serve; they're too good to burn in Hell'. The Garvies and the Hays had not realised how polonised they had become when they decided to return to Britain nearly a hundred years after their ancestors had left Scotland. Although my mother read from a Gaelic Bible every night and brought us up on Celtic legends, she never lost her foreign accent.

NOTES

1. A. E. Garvie, *Memories and Meanings of my Life*, 54.
2. S. Herbsta, *History of Żyrardów*.
3. Garvie Letters.
4. J. Naziębło, trans J Szczepanski, 'Żyrardów – a Model Industrial Town in the Time of Dittrich', in *Żyrardowski Rocznik Muzealny*, Nr 1, 1992.
5. J. C. Garvie, Lecture Notes.
6. A. E. Garvie, *op cit.*, 42–3.

CHAPTER THIRTEEN

Revolution

In 1904 Thomas Garvie started to build a new house on his estate at
Strzyzew, in 1906 he left Żyrardów, and in 1907 Strzyzew, a property
with which Scots had been associated as tenants, managers and owners
since the 1840s, was sold. For the third time in less than a hundred
years the confidence of the Scottish community was shaken by the
political upheavals of their adopted country, and many of those who
could got out. Of those who stayed, some were killed and others
ruined financially when Poland once more became a battleground
during the First World War.

The Vistula Territories were fertile ground for revolutionaries. The
most industrialised region in the Russian Empire, it was also the home
of what Norman Davies describes as 'the national movement with the
longest pedigree in Europe'. The Scots had been sympathetic to Polish
nationalism. A. E. Garvie wrote of the 1863 Rising:

> The memories of that prolonged struggle and peril were still so
> painful that I found it difficult to get my father or other older
> relatives to speak about it.[1]

But few of them had been active revolutionaries and most accepted
the programme of 'Organic Work' adopted by Polish patriots who
had survived the 1863 Rising. Their policies were dominant till the
early twentieth century when revolutionary movements again became
significant. Neal Ascherson describes their decline:

> The sober doctrines which gained support in the decades after
> the Rising, suggesting that true patriotism was to avoid head-on
> conflict with the occupiers and build up the economic and cultural
> strength of the nation by hard work, agricultural improvement
> and social organization – this cautious approach was out of fashion.[2]

But the Organic Work programme continued to dominate the thinking
of the Scots. They fitted comfortably into a growing middle class

PUNCH, OR THE LONDON CHARIVARI.—June 28, 1905.

SPORT OF THE WINDS.

(The Imperial Weather-vane.)

54. *Punch* cartoon, June 1905. Nicholas II's reactions to a revolutionary situation were dangerously inconsistent.

55. Żyrardów Tenements. Unmarried workers lived in barracks and small families in flats.

whose role in local life was being deliberately fostered by a Russian government determined to undermine the power of the aristocracy. They saw their interests 'in gradual change and reform rather than the violent upheaval of national revolution'.[3]

The 1880s and 1890s had been a period of increasing prosperity and massive economic growth. The completion of the Trans-Siberian Railway in the 1890s opened up wider eastern markets. Alarmed by the rapid industrialisation and growing power of a united Germany, Russia set out to attract foreign capital by going onto the gold standard in 1892. Money poured into the Empire from Belgium, France and Britain to finance industries where labour could still be easily exploited.

The impact on farming was insignificant. Competition from the fertile Ukraine kept prices down, and traditional markets in Britain were flooded with cheap corn grown on the American prairies. But industrialisation in Poland increased the home market. Agricultural productivity nearly doubled in the last decades of the century, from 250 million roubles in 1870 to 400 million in 1890. Scottish farming families like the Govenlocks, the Dicksons and the Hays prospered. They were sending sons to agricultural colleges in Germany and their daughters to Warsaw boarding schools for young ladies and, when they died, they could afford to erect gravestones in the Warsaw Protestant cemetery which are still impressive.

In industry the figures are more dramatic. In 1870 productivity of 114 million roubles was less than that in agriculture; by 1890 it had outstripped it and risen to 656 million.[4] The steel industry in the Dąbrowa basin had at last developed its potential but it owed more to foundations laid by Scots in the 1830s and 1840s than to any significant Scottish involvement in the second half of the century. In the cotton industry much of the technology was German; only in Żyrardów was the Scottish contribution both significant and discernible. As managers and directors the Scots helped to keep the factory in the van of technical progress; as shareholders and capitalists they were to be challenged by an international socialist movement. How successfully did they meet the challenge?

The Russian Empire was a perfect breeding ground for revolutionaries. Its educated middle class was politically powerless and provided leaders for a working class which was only slowly emerging from illiteracy. Trade unions were illegal till 1906. Professor Janzhul, a leader of the movement for reform of working conditions, is quoted as saying that 'the factory owner is an absolute sovereign and legislator whom no laws constrain'.[5] Laws which were introduced in 1887 to protect labour were modified in favour of the employers in 1893 and attempts to reduce hours to 11½ a day failed. In the cotton factories in Łódź in the 1890s the working week was 77 hours. Exploitation was normal and factory workers could be and often were flogged, humiliated and deprived of legal rights. Serfdom was not far away.

The labour movement became significant in the Empire in the 1880s; the main parties, Pilsudski's Polish Socialist Party – the PPS – and the Social Democrats, were established in the 1890s. Leadership in the factories came from the most intelligent of the workers who, unlike their counterparts in Britain, could see no prospect of emerging from poverty without revolution. As literacy spread, the masses were reached by journals – Pilsudski's *The Worker*, founded in 1894, had a circulation of 100,000 by 1899. Żyrardów, where free day and evening schools had produced a highly literate work force, was a prime target for professional revolutionaries. In 1880 an anonymous letter was found on a floor of the spinning department threatening violence to Ogden and Garvie if conditions of work and pay did not improve. The writer claimed to represent 1,248 workers.[6] A strike followed in 1883, the first in the history of the factory, but Karl Dittrich Jr was almost certainly correct in his assertion that it had been caused by foreign agitators and unemployed workers moving in from Łódź. Working and living conditions in Żyrardów were incomparably better than those in other industrial towns but paternalism did not prevent strikes. What it did do was protect Żyrardów from the worst excesses of violence when revolution swept across Russia in 1905.

Early strikes in Łódź were settled by police and troops garrisoned in the town. Agitators moved to Żyrardów which, being officially a village till 1916, had minimal policing and no military presence. Ringleaders of the 1883 strike had been brought to trial but their sentences were cancelled in the amnesty granted on the accession of Alexander III, and strikers were taken back without any loss of pay. The 1891 strike lasted only a few days but was more serious. Karl Dittrich, who had been the creative genius of the firm, had been

56. Factory Housing. Living conditions and the provision of social services were so much better than in most factory towns that Żyrardów was spared the worst violence of the revolutionary years.

succeeded by his son, another Karl. In his report to General Madern, the Russian governor in Warsaw, Dittrich suggested that a form of profit-sharing might solve some of the problems facing management:

> Another strike therefore remains a possibility as long as the difficult social conditions remain. I believe that the only way to deal with this problem is that the workers should, in some way, share in the prosperity of the factory, and this must be in a financial way. We must also persuade the workers to save money. There is no point in putting up the wages when this results in the worker spending more and striving to have a higher standard of living. There must be a compulsory savings system, so the worker spends less than he earns, and so becomes himself a capitalist. Until this happens the danger of another strike remains. And, as we can see, a strike can break out even when conditions are not bad.[7]

Peter Garvie certainly held some of these views and was an advocate of profit-sharing. He believed that the dispute was near settlement when the Russian government brought in a troop of soldiers. This, as so often happened, turned a crowd of workers into a mob, howling

A. Swan Watson   EDINBURGH.

57. Alexander Murray, *c.* 1906. The consul's son was brought up with the Garvie children. Alexander and Peter were in England for most of the revolutionary period: both boys were killed during the First World War.

for blood. Garvie pacified the demonstrators by walking out into the crowd and is reported to have said to his daughter, 'I could never have respected myself if I had shown fear'. But seventeen of the strikers were shot. Garvie was heartbroken and died the following year. His son Alfred wrote:

> ... the happy relations thus disturbed were never restored again. He seldom went for a walk beyond the garden, for the scowls he sometimes saw cut him to the heart.[8]

Under his son Thomas, earnings continued to rise in the weaving department and working hours to fall – 59½ hours a week in contrast to 77 in the cotton factories in Łódź. The firm's welfare provisions were more than doubled, adding 17% to the value of wages. As Dittrich reported in 1891:

> It is well known that such large sums spent on welfare are quite unknown in Russian factories.[9]

By 1899 he had largely withdrawn from management. He sold most of his shares and used the 680,000 roubles raised to fund a charity set up for the benefit of the workpeople. This supplemented the pensions and savings systems started by the factory. Responsibility for running the factory rested increasingly with the senior directors. When strikes again paralysed Żyrardów in 1905, action was against the government and nothing management could have done would have kept the factory going.

Russia's humiliating defeat in the 1904–05 war against Japan led to massive unemployment and political unrest. The Japanese market was lost and in Poland alone there were over 100,000 out of work. The Empire had been heading for catastrophe since the accession in 1894 of Nicholas II, a czar determined to maintain autocratic power and to resist demands, from almost every section of society, for the reforms which might have prevented revolution. By 1904 doctors, lawyers and other professionals had combined to form the Union of Unions – in effect the first trade union in Russia – and a conference of *zemstvo* local government officials demanded a representative assembly and democratic rights. On February 9th 1905 an unarmed procession of 750,000 factory workers in St Petersburg, petitioning Nicholas for protection from inhuman working conditions, was fired on by his troops. 'Bloody Sunday' destroyed the image of the czar as father of his people. Processions in Finland and Poland demanding political and national recognition spread unrest and sympathetic strikes brought the industrial economy to a standstill.

There had been very little political activity in Żyrardów between 1894 and 1904, and it was February 1905 before the factory was affected. Writing to my mother on the 29th of January, Thomas Garvie sounded determinedly optimistic:

> We are passing through very troubled times here; all Warsaw is on strike, the bakers are not baking bread, the cars and doroschas are not circulating about and the whole town is in a state of unrest. Our people are working quite quietly and we do not expect to have any trouble; the authorities also think that our work people do not intend to strike as there are no appearances of excitement among them. We are hoping to escape the agitation. As a means of precaution however there are soldiers stationed here ... there are rumours that the railway staff are all going on strike: of course the trains would then be stopped and there would be no mails possible for a few days. The whole movement cannot however last long and the interruption could not be very long.[10]

Ten days later the Żyrardów workers were on strike – 'led astray by the Warsaw people' – and interruptions lasted intermittently for a year. Young Peter and his tutor were sent to join my mother in England and old Mrs Dickson to the safety of Strzyzew, but there seems to have been almost no violence at the factory until the end of the year. The recurring refrain in the letters he wrote to reassure his children is 'the people are behaving very well and not the slightest disturbance of any kind'. There was certainly violence elsewhere. In Warsaw 100,000 workers had been on the streets and 93 had been killed by Russian troops. On January 31st he had written:

> In Warsaw things are very bad and on Saturday and Sunday the mob were allowed to break into shops and plunder them.

Of conditions in Łódź on the 26th of June, when the Żyrardów factory was back to normal working, he reported:

In Łódź there appears to be a complete state of anarchy, it is no longer a movement against the manufacturers but against the government. As the mob are now firing at the public and soldiers with revolvers, it is no wonder that they shoot in return.

There had been five days' fighting before the army restored order. But in a March letter he had written:

You must not at all accept what is printed in the newspapers as we have discovered that many of the accounts are quite untrue and many very much exaggerated. Warsaw is a manufactury of lies and the foreign correspondents believe everything told them.

My grandmother stayed with him. The tone of her letters is similar:

I can see from your letter that you are worrying. You have no reason – the workers are very polite and kind. Personally they have nothing against anybody … and only want a rise in salaries. Unfortunately this is impossible but they don't want to believe this and they hope to get something … But the misery will be very great. There are plenty of beggars – particularly women. They are asking for a piece of bread and they are very grateful if someone will give them a small piece. If the Lord will allow it this week it will finish. The Carnival was very quiet – no games, no balls, no nothing …

The renewed violence which broke out in the autumn threatened the whole Scottish community. When the leaders of the railwaymen's union were arrested, almost every railway in the country closed down and fuel and food supplies were disrupted. Industry ground to a halt and workers throughout the Empire demanded a constituent assembly and universal suffrage. Reforms reluctantly granted by the czar in the October Manifesto satisfied nobody and he retained the right to withdraw every concession he had made. But the Manifesto split the liberals and nationalists from the socialists. A Peasant Union was formed and the Social Democrats, the most active of the workers' parties, took up their cry 'All land for the peasants'. As foreign landowners, many of the Scots must have felt particularly vulnerable. In eastern Russia, where communal farming was still normal, land was seized and manor houses were burnt, but in Poland peasant farms had often been consolidated and enclosed, conditions were better and there was less violence. None of the Scots seem to have lost their land in the 1905 Revolution. Disruption of everyday life, however, affected everybody.

Jean and Peter had been allowed to come home in August but Peter was back at school in England when a general strike was called in October. Jean's letters to her brother describe conditions in Poland. On the 28th she wrote:

> If you don't hear from us for a long time please don't worry because the railways have all gone daft and we don't know if they will stop or go. To-morrow morning Mr Dernen and Mr Gruschwitz are going by horses to the Vistula and thence by steamer to Wroclavek then horses again to the frontier. Poor beggars, I don't envy them, their bones will be jolly stiff before they get home. I'm afraid Elliman's [a popular embrocation] will be in requisition ... Our people thought of striking but before they began they got a rise and now they are quite satisfied and are working well ... You have no idea what a funny feeling it is to have no papers or letters ... we might be living in the middle ages. Dolly is working at Jaktorow and can't get home. To-day the money for the workers there came and was taken by horses under escort by Cossacks. Quite romantic isn't it? ... Please don't be uneasy and think terrible things. Things are quite quiet here, bombs have been thrown in Warsaw but we know nothing. Also people say that terrible things are happening in Petersburg and Moscow they don't disturb us though. We lay in stores for some weeks, perhaps we won't be able to get much afterwards. But your pigeons will be safe. Mama will save them from being eaten. Father in factory working as hard as he can.

On the 3rd of November she wrote:

> The factory is standing because we have no coal. We light only three stoves in the house, some days there was no bread, now the butchers are to strike. In Warsaw the dry bread is about 6d a pound. We have a lot of fruit and potatoes and the Kennedy's [one of the Irish managers] oatmeal so we will manage to exist.

If it comes to the worst there are lots of rats and mice in the cellar; your pigeons will not be touched.

By November 16th only two stoves were being lit – 'My room is like an ice-box' – but trains were beginning to run again and the pigeons survived the Revolution:

Nevertheless it is jolly decent of you to offer us your pigeons. You are a regular brick.

Inevitably, during the strikes, most of the Scots identified with the industrialists; when banners were brought out of hiding on November 5th 1905 and the white Polish Eagle was displayed by thousands of workers marching through the streets of Warsaw, their sympathies were with the Poles. Herr Haupt, one of the directors, had been attacked in July and Cowdy, Kennedy and other managers and directors threatened; on Freedom Day Cowdy and Kennedy were out on the streets waving flags with the rest. But rejoicing was short-lived. My mother's description of the Żyrardów celebrations, written some years later, makes the split between the nationalists and the socialists clear. Workers from every department in the factory had marched to the church carrying their banners and singing the national anthem:[11]

The weaving, spinning, bleachworks, finishing works, dyeworks, woollen factory ... girls from the stocking factory dressed in white with myrtle wreaths on their heads carrying the Polish Eagle also decked in myrtle ... Now all the flags expected had arrived. The last one in church, the solemn thanksgiving service began. But again a company advances bearing two more flags, this time red ones; these are the Proletaryat and the Bund, the two great Socialist parties. Few cheers greet them as they advance towards the church. On the steps the flags are stopped; a deputation of workmen is standing there and refuses them entrance into the sacred building. Crestfallen, they walk back and hold an indignant meeting in the market. A table is brought, one of the Socialists mounts it and begins a most impassioned speech in Yiddish against the government, against the Czar, the directors of the factory and against everything else that stands for law and order. A few cheer the speaker, others hiss; men are getting ready for a fight. At the last moment a deputation from the workers in the church arrives asking the socialists to attend the service. Marching through the crowd they raise their war song, the Red Banner which, however, is drowned by the national anthem which the crowd strikes up. At last all was quiet and the service began.

It was to be joined later by the Jewish community:

The enthusiasm of the crowd knew no bounds. For once Jews and Christians were friends. Hundred of Jews and Jewesses crowded into the church, the former retaining their caps and attentively listened to the High Mass.[11]

Within a few weeks violence surfaced again and martial law was reimposed. In Russia, before the promised Duma opened in April 1906, 15,000 people were executed, 20,000 were shot or wounded and 45,000 exiled. Thomas Garvie was reported to be on the revolutionaries' hit list and narrowly escaped assassination. By the end of November my mother was back with her relations in London; by the end of the year her parents were spending Christmas in Berlin, refused permission by the Russian authorities to return to Poland. Writing from a board meeting in mid-December, Garvie had reported:

From Żyrardów we hear that the people are restless and on Wednesday they tried by force to get into the head office, they were however driven back by the guard and when the Cossacks came riding up they at once dispersed.

It was the end of January before the directors were allowed to return to Żyrardów. There had been no attacks on their houses and in the factory damage was limited to that caused by pipes freezing when coal supplies ran out. But it had been a terrible year. The two senior directors, Haupt and Garvie, had taken turns to be in residence to deal with the recurring crises. They were both worn out. On the 30th of December Thomas wrote to my mother:

I hope that before another year has passed away we may be all settled down in Britain and that on the New Year's Day we may be together in our new home.

Paternalism had almost certainly saved Żyrardów from the appalling violence which had swept across Russia. The American consul in Batumi described the country in the autumn of 1905:

> Permeated with sedition and reeking with revolution, racial hatred and warfare, incendiarism, brigandage, robbery and crime of every kind.[12]

There were more strikes in Poland than in the whole of the rest of the Empire but fewer in Żyrardów than in other industrial towns. From retirement in Dresden in 1907 Dittrich wrote:

> The thought that the influence of the church, the kindergarten and the school which have always been the subjects of my particular efforts perhaps prevented more bitter results of the movement [1905] makes me particularly happy.

The Scots had helped to create a community in which hatred did not engulf managers and proprietors; their own servants had protected them from assassination. Where they appear to have failed was in their inability to understand the gravity of the issues which remained. But perhaps one should not assess Garvie's political judgment by letters written to reassure his children. His decision to leave Poland is more significant.

NOTES

1. A. E. Garvie, *Memories and Meanings of my Life*, 30.
2. N. Ascherson, *The Struggle for Poland*, 14.
3. *Ibid*, 15.
4. I. Kostrowicka, Changes in Agricultural Productivity, 82, in *Journal of European Economic History*, XIII.
5. O. Figes, *A People's Tragedy*, 114.
6. K. Dittrich, Report on the 1891 Strike at Żyrardów.
7. *Ibid*, 62.
8. A. E. Garvie, *op cit.*, 62.
9. K. Dittrich, *op cit*.
10. Garvie Letters.
11. J. C. Garvie, Papers.
12. O. Figes, *op cit.*, 188.

CHAPTER FOURTEEN

War

The gap between those Scots who accepted assimilation into Polish society and those who were determined to remain Scottish had been widening since the mid-nineteenth century. Had the Congress Kingdom, which had seemed so full of promise in 1815, been allowed to develop its independence under a Russian king, it might have won the loyalty of the immigrant Scots. The Revolution of 1905, although it forced the Russian government to recognise the existence of Poland as a nation, did nothing to close the gap. Confidence had been destroyed.

Within a few weeks of Freedom Day the czar launched a regime which Orlando Figes describes as 'a reign of terror' and Count Witte, the most enlightened of his ministers, considered 'brutal and excessive and often totally unjustified'. By the time the Duma met in May 1906 Polish representation had been cut from the promised 36 to 14, but there were some real reforms. Trade unions became legal in 1906 and locally elected councils were set up in the country in 1911 and in the cities by 1913. The press and the use of the Polish language were less savagely repressed. By 1912 the economy was recovering from the loss of the Japanese market. Polish goods were reaching Turkey, Persia and China and government policies favoured industrialists as a counterweight to the aristocracy. My mother believed that had war not broken out, Russia might have moved peacefully towards a form of limited democracy.

The farming community continued to invest in land. Strzyzew was sold but the Dicksons bought another farm on land which, in 1997, was still called Diksonowa. Peter Hay, who had inherited his father's Polish estate, bought another at Prijutino, near Smolensk in Russia. Life appeared to be going on normally. Vincent Hoser, a successful Warsaw florist and nurseryman, invested in an estate near Ciechocinek. In July 1914 his wife, Margaret Garvie, was in Warsaw buying a new mowing machine in preparation for what was

58. Hielle & Dittrich letter heading, 1911. After his retirement from management in 1906 Thomas Garvie attended board meetings in Berlin or Żyrardów every two months. The language of management was German.

expected to be an exceptionally good harvest. The Garvies had left Żyrardów but there was a wide range of family houses in the country as well as in Warsaw where they could stay in comfort during their frequent visits to Poland. In town the language might still be English; in the country it was more likely to have become Polish and children to be called Jerzy and Małgorzata instead of George and Margaret.

It was in Żyrardów that the break was clearly evident. For the first time, none of the 'Swiss Style' houses built by Hielle & Dittrich for their senior personnel was occupied by a Garvie or a Hay. But the factory continued to grow and Thomas Garvie to play a significant part in its development. To do this involved endless travelling. Hotel letter headings paint a charming picture of the Europe in which he was travelling for pleasure as well as on business. In 1908 the 'Hotel & Badhaus zum Schwarzen Bock' at Wiesbaden boasted central heating, electric light and a telephone for its 150 rooms; the 'Grand Union Hotel, Dresden' in 1908 advertised rooms with bath and toilet and a garage for cars as well as stabling for horses. There are carriages, horse buses, cyclists, an electric tram and one motor car in the illustration

59.   Grand Union Hotel, Dresden. The Dittrichs retired to Dresden in 1907. On his frequent visits, Garvie stayed at a hotel which boasted garaging and a telephone as well as stabling for horses.

of the Bismarkplatz in which the hotel stood. In the letters there are constant references to continuing work. There were visits to the exhibition in Brussels, to factories in Dundee, Belfast and Manchester and private meetings with other directors in Dresden, Cologne and St Petersburg as well as the formal board meetings in Berlin. Increasingly, my homesick grandmother went abroad with him, prolonging her visits to relatives in Poland while my grandfather returned to spend holidays with his family in Scotland.

If the board meetings, usually six a year, were held in Berlin, they would be followed by visits to Żyrardów. In July 1911 he complained:

> I cannot be long here but people begin appealing to me verbally or by letter for protection, women wanting pensions wish me to confirm all kinds of cock and bull stories about things that happened thirty years ago.[1]

International socialist organisation and industrial unrest increased throughout Europe in the years preceding the Great War. In 1910 he wrote:

> Everything appears to be very quiet and peaceful at present among the work people. There have been a number of arrests of socialists within the last two months and this I suppose will have made a certain impression.

But by February 1913 there were strikes in the weaving department, which had always been the Garvies' chief concern:

> They have been obliged to lock out the workers in one of the departments of weaving and it is now standing and my presence will be very necessary.

The dispute was settled and the factory was still expanding in 1914. To the concert hall and club rooms Karl Dittrich added a theatre for the workers, and Garvie was involved in the design of a new weaving complex. On July 6th he wrote from Żyrardów:

> I expect to be here all day and to-morrow and expect to be very busy as I have a good deal to do with the new weaving shed which is being built.

Neither the industrialists nor the farmers expected the War. Within a few months German troops had occupied Żyrardów, and the corn the farmers had hoped to harvest was being trampled into the ground by invading armies. By the end of the war the factory was in ruins.

On August 1st 1914 Thomas was recalled from a family holiday in Perthshire to attend an emergency board meeting in Berlin. When Britain declared war, he was put under house arrest and his bank account was frozen. He was unable to communicate with his family, but, being over military age, he was repatriated in October. In midwinter he returned to Poland to rescue the firm from total disaster. War had closed the normal route through Germany and, until a rail link was built between Finland and Russia, part of the journey had to be made by sledge. On the grounds that Hielle and Dittrich were Austrians and the firm's headquarters were in Berlin, the Russian government had confiscated its assets and started to move trainloads of valuable machinery to Russia. Garvie proved that over a third of the shareholders were either British or French. He re-formed the company under a Russian chairman and, by excluding all enemy aliens, forced the Russian government to pay adequate compensation for what had been taken.

In his letters it becomes 'our company'. In January 1915 he had written from Copenhagen describing emergency efforts to help the workers in Żyrardów. A week later my grandmother, who had always been considered 'nervous and delicate', set out on her own to join him. She left a grey London winter behind her, and the tone of her letter suggests an exile returning home. She wrote from a train making its slow way through Sweden and Finland to Russia:

> There is about one metre of snow and I felt better when I saw trees covered with hoar frost. Narrow lanes are cleared to the houses. A lot of the forests are almost under the snow and of fences only the tops can be seen. They are looking like great white mushrooms.

The Germans had been driven back from Warsaw in 1914 but by July 1915 re-occupied the whole of Russian Poland. The Garvies retreated to Moscow and Thomas spent the rest of his life in Russia, selling off the company's assets. In a letter to his wife in November 1915 he describes what had to be done:

> I have to-day finally come to an agreement with the representative of the Russian linen manufacturers that they are to take over all our new Russian flaxes at a price which will give us a fair profit. Our flax yarns are now also disposed off. I have now only our cotton yarns which a new commission are now sorting out and valuing. After this has been sorted there will only be some smaller items left, such as half-finished goods which I am getting gradually finished and when ready get them sold through our shops. It will in any case take a few months to get everything cleared up. I have not had time till now to look after the shops but I suppose it will be necessary for me later to pay visits to our branch businesses in Charkow, Odessa etc and to decide what we are to do with them when there are no more goods to sell. I suppose it will be necessary to close them up and dismiss our shop men.

PUNCH, OR THE LONDON CHARIVARI.—November 15, 1905.

THE ELEVENTH HOUR.

of King Louis the Sixteenth (*to the* Czar). " SIDE WITH YOUR PEOPLE, SIRE, WHILE THERE IS YET TIME. *I* WAS TOO LATE ! "

60. *Punch* cartoon, November 1905. The warning which Czar Nicholas II ignored.

I have had no news of any kind from Żyrardów since you left; have you not heard from Janka [her sister, Janet Dickson]?

When their only son Peter was killed in June 1917, he was still in Moscow and hoped that his wife would be able to join him. He wrote in July:

> It is quite impossible for me to get away from here now. Our chairman Count W was getting a little better from his first paralytic stroke but last week got much worse again so it is quite impossible for him to do anything in connection with the business. Everything now depends upon me.

On August 27th he was still optimistic about the political situation. He knew that other members of the Scottish circle who were refugees in Russia were being ferried back to Britain in escorted convoys and could not understand why permission was refused for his wife to come out on a returning convoy. To his daughter he wrote:

> I am very sorry your mother has not been able to join me here ... our authorities must have special reasons for their prohibition.

61. Warsaw shop. One of the firm's many retail shops which Garvie had to close
down when he wound up the business in 1918.

62. Żyrardów, 1918. The Germans destroyed the factory before they were driven
out of Poland in 1918.

Things are pretty unsettled here but I am not as pessimistic as
some people and hope that things will right themselves in course
of time.

During the October Revolution he had to go into hiding, sheltered
by a Jewish family in Moscow, and it was July 1918 before he was
able to set off for home. Eastern currencies had maintained their value
and he had salvaged the equivalent of £300,000 for the firm. But civil
war was destroying Russia. He reached Murmansk, where Britain had
established a naval base, but died before he could board the ship which
would have taken him back to Britain. Every rouble he had recovered
for the company and for his extended family was lost in the turmoil
of the Bolshevik revolution.

In Żyrardów the factory had been seriously damaged but the hospital
survived and Janet Dickson stayed on as its matron. As children we
used to love to hear of her exploits during the War. As well as
employing the local thieves to recover drugs and equipment stolen by
the occupying Germans, she herself forged the entries on stolen birth

certificates in order to protect Poles from conscription into the German army. Another Scot, a cousin of my mother's, used to ride past a prison camp every night. Knowing that the prisoners were starving, she used to canter past, standing in her stirrups and throwing bread she had hidden under her habit over the wire fence.

Of those who stayed on, some were killed and many ruined. Peter Hay got back to Poland but lost everything he had invested in his Russian estate. His sister Catherine Hay saved her husband Carl Hannich from execution. As an Austrian citizen, a director of Hielle & Dittrich and the possessor of one of the few private telephones in Warsaw, he was suspected of espionage. Making contact with the English wife of one of the Russian generals for whom houses were being requisitioned, Catherine persuaded the General and his family to take over the Hannich home. Telling the story in St Albans 85 years later, her daughter Nulla said the General was charmed by her mother into getting the sentence commuted to exile. Catherine and her children moved to the Hay estate in Russia and then followed Hannich to Siberia. All his property was confiscated, but the family survived on Catherine's, protected by her British passport and Polish law under which married women retained their own property. Some Scots moved east to escape the Germans and disappeared in the Civil War, others reached Britain as penniless refugees. The Dicksons sold land and lost everything in the galloping inflation of the postwar years. The McLeod who had become a Machlejd survived the First but was killed in the Second World War. Those who had married Germans and identified with Germany got out.

In the late 1870s the second generation of Garvies was still ambivalent about nationality. Peter had planned to return to Scotland and Thomas was sent to Glasgow to set up a linen factory at Bridgeton in which he and his brother Alfred would have been in partnership with their father. When Alfred decided that he must study for the ministry, the plan was dropped and Thomas returned to Żyrardów. Peter decided to stay in Poland and applied for Russian citizenship. His application was rejected.[2] A few years later the government changed its policy. Russian nationality was offered to foreigners in salaried posts and expulsion threatened if they did not apply for naturalisation. Thomas, then a manager in the factory, led the foreigners in Żyrardów in refusing to accept the offer. The Governor of Poland, realising that expulsion of 70% of its senior personnel would have led to the closure of the factory and the loss of thousands of jobs, sensibly and quietly allowed the order to drop.[3] The third generation of Garvies had made their position clear: they were prepared to work in Poland only if they could retain their British passports and their Scottish roots. In the Republic of Poland which emerged after the War there was no place for divided loyalties. The Scots who stayed on became Poles.

NOTES

1. Garvie Letters.
2. Dittrich Report, 1891.
3. A. E. Garvie, *Memories and Meanings of My Life*, 35.

CHAPTER FIFTEEN

Agents of Change?

It was 1993 before I visited Poland and began to understand why my grandmother had loved the country and its people while my mother rejected them. Warsaw, rebuilt by a nation which refused to die, was full of ghosts; Żyrardów seemed a ghost town. I wandered through its empty streets on a hot and dusty Sunday afternoon, finding no one who could speak enough English or French to tell me what was happening in the semi-derelict factory buildings or who lived in the gaunt brick houses. I returned to Warsaw and the tourist trail to Cracow and Zakopane, using my 'Beginners' Course' Polish for survival but learning little about the Scots in Poland in the nineteenth century. It was only at Kielce University that some of my questions were answered by an academic with whom I had been put in touch by the Polish consul-general in Edinburgh. He was the first of a number of historians who have been outstandingly generous in making their research available to me. Without them the Polish side of the picture would have been almost totally dependent on family papers.

The destruction wreaked by two wars and the repeated occupation of the country by German and Russian troops has been devastating. With courage and grim determination the Poles have restored buildings deliberately destroyed by their enemies; the generation of educated men and women, equally ruthlessly eliminated, was irreplaceable. For 50 years, Polish children have been taught politically 'correct' history and studied at universities under politically acceptable lecturers. The role of Polish aristocrats and of the foreign technicians and capitalists they attracted to the country, in stimulating the development of the economy in the nineteenth century, has not been widely studied. And one suspects that the extent to which development was retarded by Russian policies has not been fully explored. Valuable work in these fields has only recently been done by Polish historians, some of whom have been able to study in British universities.

What did the Scots achieve? My first impressions were negative.

63. Two Million Mark Note. Russian, German and Polish currencies held their value until 1920. By 1923 galloping inflation ruined many of the Scots who had survived the War.

Much of the land is still farmed by methods I associate with farming in Scotland between the wars. There were 20 horses for every tractor and a dozen workers, men, women and children, could be seen returning to the fields after the dinner break. There were no combines operating in the wheat fields and corn was being stooked as it had been 50 years ago in Scotland. Rose Lehman, a garden historian visiting Poland in 1987, described similar scenes:

> Speeding south-east from Warsaw ... one is immediately aware of the extreme rurality of Poland. Horse drawn vehicles every-where, a woman washing clothes in a tin bath in her garden amongst rugosa roses; some nuns at Klemensów, [formerly one of the great palaces] now a home for the elderly and disabled, haymaking ... Cottage gardens with neat rows of vegetables; a mass of flowers ... And behind the houses little farmyards with turkeys, geese and hens, then strip cultivation of fields by hand or horse power, a tethered Friesian cow or two ...[1]

Little had changed in the early 1990s. Heavy carts, intended for two horses, were often being drawn by one and the light and efficient two-wheeled carts introduced by the Scots had disappeared. But hay and corn were being stored in the open in stacks like the ones I had been taught to build in the 1940s. These make the huge barns which were a characteristic of Polish farms in the early nineteenth century unnecessary. Potatoes, introduced by the Scots as a field crop, were being protected from winter frost by straw and earth as they would have been in Scotland. They have become a staple part of the Polish diet as well as the main ingredient in vodka.

Farmhouses can still be as primitive as the Scottish farm labourers' homes of the 1940s. In one in which I was generously entertained, three generations – nine people – were living in a four-apartment wooden house, their only water supply drawn from a well in the courtyard and their only lavatory shared with cows in the byre. At Strzyzew, the two-storey brick houses built by the Garvies for their employees have been replaced by bungalows on the smallholdings into which the estate was divided in 1946. Under-capitalised and often technically under-educated farmers rarely introduce advanced technologies, and both living conditions and farming methods seemed to be 50 years behind those in the west. Productivity is lamentably low for a country which was once the granary of northern Europe.

Massive investment and reorganisation of landholding are again needed if standards are to be raised, but this in no way invalidates the significance of the contribution made by Scots to the development of farming nearly 200 years ago. Observing Scottish farms in the late eighteenth and early nineteenth centuries, Polish landowners realised that their own estates could be made more productive. Under Scottish professors they studied current theories of agriculture, and from farmers like Muir in Galloway and Rennie in East Lothian they learnt some of the necessary skills. Their mentors were Adam Smith, Sir John Sinclair and J C Loudon. Armed with textbooks and encyclopaedias, they returned to Poland to transform their estates. The farmers they recruited brought with them technologies which were the most advanced in Europe. That they could be profitably applied to farming in Poland was demonstrated at agricultural shows on the great estates and publicised in journals and by societies. The suppression of the societies and exile of their leaders after the two failed Risings were an economic as well as a political tragedy which checked the spread of improved farming.

This in its turn had a similar effect on the work of the engineers. The machines they made were good but in a country where serfdom

64. The Polish Cart, 1995. Agriculture lagging behind western Europe – back to the four-wheeled cart.

was not abolished until the 1860s there was little incentive for unenterprising landowners to mechanise their farms. Labour was cheap and machines expensive. The market for agricultural machinery remained small and when Lilpop, the Polish engineer trained by the Evans brothers, invented an improved reaper in 1863, he sold the patent to Ransome & Sim in England. There were no tariffs to protect the work of Polish inventors and too few incentives to develop new machines. The primitive three-field system dominated Polish agriculture until well into the second half of the century; land lay fallow and farmers continued to scratch the soil and understock their farms. The machines which were essential for better cultivation and harvesting were rarely ordered. The frequency of financial failure amongst those who set up engineering firms, either on their own or with Polish or Scottish partners, was due to limited markets and under-capitalisation rather than incompetence. The quality of their work has not been questioned. Two Meikle threshing machines built at Dowspuda in 1817 were still in use 45 years later, as were many of the machines and steam engines with which they equipped ancillary industries.[2] Most important, they conveyed their skills to Polish apprentices. To quote Niziol:

> The factories of Solec and Białogen were founded, laying a firm foundation for a tradition of excellence in machine construction which was to be the main lasting legacy of British technology to the Kingdom.[3]

At Białogon and Zwierzyniec some of the factories they set up and managed are still operating.

Historians have been more critical of the work of the foreign metallurgists. The creation of a vast smelting plant at Dąbrowa, where the Silesian coal proved to be unsuitable for coking, was clearly an economic disaster. But men like Preacher and Watson had been employed by the Bank Polski to introduce the most advanced techniques; they were not consulted about their appropriateness for Polish conditions in the 1830s and 1840s. Nor were they responsible for the long delay in the development of the railway network which would have created a market for steel and made the use of ore from eastern Poland economically viable. The plant they installed was developed

65. Dowspuda, 1995. The house which was once at the heart of General Pac's great experiments in engineering, industry and farming. See p. 57.

66. Strzyzew. The ruins of the house that Garvie built in 1904.

successfully by French industrialists who bought up the government blast furnaces in 1876. The Scots had contributed to the transfer of technologies and trained a generation of Polish workers; again, the foundations they laid had been sound.

The work of the gardeners is still visible. In creating romantic gardens they altered the landscape. The lakes and mounds and meandering rivers are still there, as well as many of the magnificent trees. Lehman described those she saw in 1987:

> The parks we had come to see were mostly in a state of gentle decay and the feeling of lost demesne pervaded. Under grass smothered in dandelion clocks, buttercups, the Mourning Widow cranesbill, delicate campanulas, ragged robin, a truly flowery mead. In perfect summer weather we strolled under towering lime avenues, idled along partially silted up moats and lakes full of yellow flag iris and white horseradish ... accompanied by the croaking of bull frogs, the fluting of Golden Oriels and attacks by mosquitoes. Finding the features and follies we were seeking; Chinese pavillions in variety; by the lake at Koscielec a mosque and minaret as well as a castle ruin. At Kruszynaa a very exciting

'Hermitage Complex' appeared through the undergrowth – a small building (one a chapel and one a bakery) on each of the four corners of the surrounding walls entered under a domed portico.[4]

When I visited Dowspuda the lake had silted up and the gates of the weir had rusted but great avenues of lime trees still lead to the ruined house and radiate from its empty rooms. The avenue at Strzyzew has been blocked by a fire station, but what is left of the house is surrounded by roses, and the park and the trees my mother climbed are still there.

I have only been able to find one of my relatives who speaks fluent English. With her help I was able to return to Żyrardów in 1995 as the guest of the curator of the regional museum. There was still a small linen firm operating in one corner of the huge factory complex; by 1997 it was in liquidation. Between the Wars the factory had been partially rebuilt and then bought by a French firm. It employed less than a quarter of the previous workforce. The managers lived in Warsaw and, after several years of poor labour relations and the production of shoddy goods which undermined Żyrardów's reputation for excellence, the firm was prosecuted for tax evasion. When A. E. Garvie visited his old home in 1925 he found that the directors' park, which his father had opened to the workers, had again been locked. An old employee he met shook his head when questioned about conditions. 'The old gentleman was a good soul, the young gentleman was a good soul, but now ...' He left the sentence unfinished.[5] The firm was taken over by the government and resold, only to be overwhelmed by the devastation of the Second World War. Synthetic fabrics and the relative poverty of eastern European markets have done the rest.

On the last day of his visit in 1925 Alfred's sister-in-law Janet Dickson, still matron of the hospital, drove him out to see the family graves in the Protestant cemetery at Wiskitki. Although German and Russian armies had fought over the ground eight times, the graves were undamaged except by age. When I visited them in 1997 I could find only one unbroken and recognisable stone. The Scots had been buried beside the Protestant Germans and in 1945 their graves had been desecrated and destroyed along with those of the enemy.

67. Jean Garvie, *c.* 1914. My mother, from whose papers I started my search for the Scots in Poland.

In Żyrardów itself the bones of the model industrial town they had helped to build still exist. The Protestants are back into the hall in which they had originally worshipped, and a Catholic congregation uses the church Dittrich built for them in the 1890s. The schools, the hospital, the fire station, the theatre and the parks still exist. The streets are tree-lined, the managers' club is a restaurant and the 'Important Visitors'' office a museum. Six families now live in the house in which my mother grew up and neither it nor the cottages and barracks built for the workers would be considered acceptable accommodation now. But in its day it was a factory and a town of which the directors could be justifiably proud. It was only when I saw a panoramic view, painted in 1890, that I realised how vast the complex had been. Photos in the museum's archives created a picture of a community which was more than an industrial town. The Dittrich period had become a legend and the Scots had made a major contribution to its creation. I understood why my grandmother returned to Poland every possible year until 1939, when war and old age made the journey impossible for her.

The doctors, nurses, teachers, bankers and veterinary scientists have left fewer tangible monuments behind them. But in a century when Russian policies destroyed the educational foundations necessary for the development of a professional middle class, their contacts with the west must have made their contribution to the economic and social life of Poland significant.

My grandmother idealised the Poland she had had to leave; my mother the Scotland to which she longed to return. They are buried beside each other in a graveyard in the Borders, in country so many of their ancestors had known and loved. I have tried to tell their story and the story of the Scottish community of which they were a part before all record of their achievements disappear.

NOTES

1. R. Lehman, in *Garden History Newsletter*, 18, 5.
2. S. Niziol, *British Technologies and Polish Economic Development, 1815–63*.
3. *Ibid.*
4. R. Lehman, *ibid*, 5.
5. A. E. Garvie, *Memories and Meanings of My Life*, 204.

Bibliography

PRIMARY

Dittrich, K. Memorandum explaining reasons for a strike of the Żyrardów factory workers on 1st, 2nd, and 4th of May 1891.

Foreign Office Records, Consular Reports 1834–75.

Garvie Letters, 1864–1917.

Garvie Memoirs and Papers.

Girard Archives, Lourmarin, France.

Hay Letters, 1819–64.

Hay Memoirs.

Kedslie Notebooks.

National Archives, Suwałki, Poland.

SECONDARY

Anderson, I. G., *Scotsmen in the Service of the Czar*, Edinburgh (1990).

Ascherson, N., *The Struggle for Poland*, London (1987).

Bremner, D., *The Industries of Scotland*, Edinburgh (1867).

Burton, J. H., *The Scots Abroad*, Edinburgh (1861).

Butt, J., *The Industrial Archaeology of Scotland*, Newton Abbot (1967).

Cage, R. A. (ed.), *The Scots Abroad*, London (1985).

Campbell, R. H., *Scotland Since 1707*, Edinburgh (1992).

Clough, M., *Two Houses*, Aberdeen (1990).

Cumming, G. & Devine, T. M. (eds), *Industry, Business and Society in Scotland since 1700*, Edinburgh (1994).

David, A., *Scottish Linen Industries in the Eighteenth Century*, Edinburgh (1979).

Davies, N., *God's Playground, A History of Poland*, Oxford (1981).

Davies, N., *Heart of Europe. A short History of Poland*, Oxford (1984).

Davies, N., *Europe. A History*, Oxford (1996).

Fedorowiezed, J. K. (ed.), *A Republic of Nobles. Studies in Polish History to 1864*, Cambridge (1992).

Fenton, A., *Scottish Country Life*, Edinburgh (1976).

Figes, O., *A People's Tragedy: The Russian Revolution, 1891–1924*, London (1996).

Fischer, T. A., *The Scots in Germany*, Edinburgh (1902).

Garvie, A. E., *Memories and Meanings of my Life*, London (1938).

Gauldie, E., *The Scottish Country Miller, 1700–90*, Edinburgh (1981).

Gauldie, E., *Spinning and Weaving*, Edinburgh (1995).

Graham, I. I. C., *Colonists from Scotland, 1707–83*, Cornell.

Lenman, B., *Integration, Enlightenment and Industrialization: Scotland 1746–1832*, London (1981).

Louden, J. C., *Enclyclopaedia of Agriculture*, London (1831).

Mitchison, R., *Agricultural Sir John: The Life of Sir John Sinclair of Ulbster 1754–1835*, London (1962).

Murray, N., *The Scottish Handloom Weavers, 1790–1850*, Edinburgh (1978).

Niziol, S. British Technology and Polish Economic Development 1815–63, (unpublished Ph.D. thesis, London School of Economics, 1995).

Pares, B., *A History of Russia*, London (1958).

Reilly, V., *Paisley Pattern*, Glasgow (1987).

Sinclair, J., *Statistical Account of Scotland 1791–99*, (ed. Witherspoon, D. J. and Grant, I. R.) Vols II, III, IX, Wakefield (1975–9).

Sinclair, J., *Analysis of the Statistical Account of Scotland*, Edinburgh (1825).

Smout, T. C., *History of the Scottish People, 1560–1830*, London (1969).

Smout, T. C., *A Century of the Scottish People, 1830–1950*, London (1986).

Smout, T. C (ed.), *Scotland and Europe, 1200–1850*, Edinburgh (1986).

Sprott, G., *Farming*, Edinburgh (1995).

Stephen, H., *The Book of the Farm*, 2nd edn, Edinburgh (1851).

Steuart, A. F., *Papers Relating to the Scots in Poland, 1576–1793*, Scottish History Society Vol. LIX, Edinburgh (1915).

Thompson, D., *Europe since Napoleon*, Harmondsworth (1967).

Topham, E., *Letters from Edinburgh, 1774–75*, Edinburgh (1971).

Wormell, S., *Palas Poland*, London (1994).

Zamoyski, A., *The Polish Way*, London (1987).

Zamoyski, A., *The Last King of Poland*, London (1992).

ARTICLES

Bartyś, J. 'English and Scottish Farmers in Poland in the first half of the Nineteenth Century', *Agricultural History Review*, Vol. XV (1967).

Cross, A. 'Russian Gardens, British Gardeners', in *Garden History*, vol. 19, 1 (1991).

Knox, B., 'The Arrival of the English Landscape Garden in Poland and Bohemia', in *The Picturesque Garden and its Influence outside the British Isles*, Dumbarton Oaks (1974).

Kostrowicka, I., 'Changes in Agricultural Productivity in the Kingdom of Poland in the Nineteenth and early Twentieth Centuries', *The Journal of European Economic History*, Vol. XIII (1984).

Liponski, W. (ed.), *Polish-AngloSaxon Studies*, vols 1, 2, 6–7 (1987, 1991, 1997).

Stawarz, A. and Wozniak A., 'From Ethnographic Studies on Workers' Cultures in the Nineteenth and Beginning of the Twentieth Century. Żyrardów, Centre of the Textile Industry', in *Ethnologia Polona*, vol. 10, 1984, 39–89.

Zytkowiez, L., 'The Peasant's Farm and the Landlord's Farm from the Sixteenth to the mid Eighteenth Centuries', *The Journal of European Economic History*, vol. I, 1972.

POLISH SECONDARY

Herbsta, S. *Historya Żyrardowski 1830–70* (1985).

Fijalkowski, P. '120 lat zboru w Żyrardowie' (1995).

Goralski, A., 'Cudzoziemcy w Żyrardowie na Przelomie XIX i XX Wieku', Żyrardów (1980).

Nażiebło, J (ed.), *Żyrardowski Rocznik Muzealny vols 1, 2, 3,* Żyrardów (1992–95).

Radzysewski, H., *Bank Polski,* Poznan (1919).

Stawarz, A., *Żyrardów Narodziny Spotecznosci,* Żyrardów (1985).

Szczepański, J., *Modernizacja Górnictwa i Hutnictwa w Królestwie Polskim w i Polowie XIX W. Rola Specjalistow Niemieckich i Brytyjskich,* Kielce (1997).

Szyrma, K. L., *Anglia i Szkocja: Przypomnienia z 1820–24 odbytej,* Warsaw (1829).

Genealogical Tables

THE HAYS

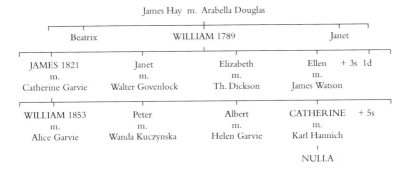

James Hay m. Arabella Douglas

Beatrix	WILLIAM 1789	Janet

JAMES 1821 m. Catherine Garvie	Janet m. Walter Govenlock	Elizabeth m. Th. Dickson	Ellen m. James Watson	+ 3s 1d

WILLIAM 1853 m. Alice Garvie	Peter m. Wanda Kuczynska	Albert m. Helen Garvie	CATHERINE m. Karl Hannich	+ 5s

NULLA

THE GARVIES

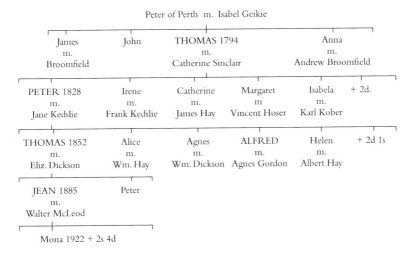

Peter of Perth m. Isabel Geikie

James m. Broomfield	John	THOMAS 1794 m. Catherine Sinclair	Anna m. Andrew Broomfield

PETER 1828 m. Jane Kedslie	Irene m. Frank Kedslie	Catherine m. James Hay	Margaret m Vincent Hoser	Isabela m. Karl Kober	+ 2d.

THOMAS 1852 m. Eliz. Dickson	Alice m. Wm. Hay	Agnes m. Wm. Dickson	ALFRED m. Agnes Gordon	Helen m. Albert Hay	+ 2d 1s

JEAN 1885 m. Walter McLeod	Peter

Mona 1922 + 2s 4d

THE KEDSLIES

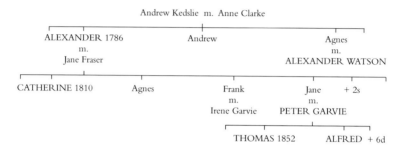

Andrew Kedslie m. Anne Clarke

ALEXANDER 1786   Andrew   Agnes
m.   m.
Jane Fraser   ALEXANDER WATSON

CATHERINE 1810   Agnes   Frank   Jane   + 2s
m.   m.
Irene Garvie   PETER GARVIE

THOMAS 1852   ALFRED + 6d

THE DICKSONS

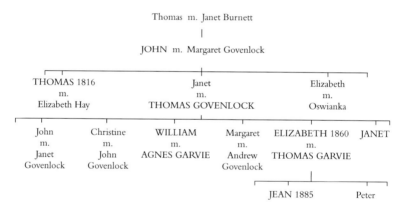

Thomas m. Janet Burnett

JOHN m. Margaret Govenlock

THOMAS 1816   Janet   Elizabeth
m.   m.   m.
Elizabeth Hay   THOMAS GOVENLOCK   Oswianka

John   Christine   WILLIAM   Margaret   ELIZABETH 1860   JANET
m.   m.   m.   m.   m.
Janet   John   AGNES GARVIE   Andrew   THOMAS GARVIE
Govenlock Govenlock   Govenlock

JEAN 1885   Peter

THE GOVENLOCKS

Walter, 1795, Robert, and a third brother were amongst the earliest tenants on the Dowspuda estate. They intermarried with their cousins and with other Scottish families and repeatedly used the same Christian names for their children. I have been unable to disentangle the exact relationships of Peter, a director of Heille & Dittrich, and his wife Helen, or of Janka, who worked for my parents in the 1920s.

INTERMARRIAGE

Within two generations six families had intermarried 26 times. I know too little about families like the Watsons, the Broomfields and the

Heitons to include them separately. Characters who are prominent in the text appear in capital letters. Marriages outside the Protestant or Scottish circle become commoner by the end of the century.

Index

Note: Page numbers in *italic* refer to illustrations. There may also be textual references on these pages.